BUILT TO
LEAD,
BUILT TO
SCALE

How Modern Leaders
Turn Businesses into Platforms

Built to Lead, Built to Scale
How Modern Leaders Turn Businesses into Platforms

Jason Mickool

Published by Game Changer Publishing

Paperback ISBN: 979-8-90158-136-0
Hardcover ISBN: 979-8-90158-137-7
Digital ISBN: 979-8-90158-138-4

www.GameChangerPublishing.com

To my wife and family—you are the reason behind every risk I've taken and every dream I've chased. Your belief in me never wavered, even when the vision was bigger than the resources. This book exists because of your love, patience, and constant encouragement.

To the leaders who believed in me before I fully believed in myself—thank you for investing your time, your wisdom, and your standards into my development. You didn't just teach strategy; you shaped my character. You modeled what leadership looks like when it's rooted in integrity and courage.

This book is my attempt to pass forward what you so generously gave to me.

ADVANCE PRAISE

"If you want real substance on business methodology, bring Jason in to speak. Your people will walk away with an expansive mindset. There are 500,000+ people in the world who call themselves coaches. Most have never built what they coach on, let alone at the pace and intensity that Jason Mickool has. Jason is one of the few practitioners who has actually built what he teaches, which is building, growing, scaling, and exiting at a rapid pace. In over 35 years of coaching high-performance organizations, I have never seen the training and development arm like Jason has created. Six hundred and fifty to eight hundred young people dialed in to a true development system. It's a magical thing to watch."

Coach Burt
Founder, The Greatness Factory

"Jason is a true leader, someone who not only understands the financial services industry at a deep and meaningful level but knows how to translate that knowledge into real growth… In my entire career, I have never seen a firm grow in every single measure the way that Florida Financial Advisors has."

Mike Vietri
Chief Distribution Officer for AmeriLife

"Jason is not your typical speaker. His no-fluff, no-nonsense approach is backed by real systems and real processes. He teaches from a place of doing, not theory, and challenges people to expand how they think and execute."

Chase Gruening
Founder & CEO of GHW GRUENING

Read This First

Just to say thanks for buying and reading my book,
I would like to connect with you!

Scan the QR Code here.

BUILT TO
LEAD,
BUILT TO
SCALE

How Modern Leaders
Turn Businesses into Platforms

JASON MICKOOL

FOREWORD

After 35+ years of coaching other people, I thought I had seen just about everything in business until I was asked to do a Zoom coaching session for Jason Mickool's company, Florida Financial Advisors. The person who made the introduction said to me, "You've probably never seen anything like this." I thought, *Try me, because I've seen just about everything.* Boy, was I wrong.

What I saw was abnormal in today's world when I showed up to coach, which was over 600+ young and hungry people, who all looked like somebody and were ready to hang on every word I said. They were hungry, humble, and teachable. They were alert, curious, and responsive. I knew that someone had to orchestrate this. Someone who had to be an expert at recruiting, training, and developing people.

Most founders create jobs rather than build businesses. It's not that they don't want to build a business that can be grown, scaled, and sold; they just don't believe they can, or they don't know how. This is where Jason Mickool thrives: crushing limiting beliefs and showing people step by step how to actually build a real business that has big profits and real value. He creates a platform where all involved expand in a positive-expectancy environment.

In my short time with Jason, he's challenged the way I think about recruiting and scaling. He's grown my "production capacity intelligence." (Yes, I made this intelligence up.) He's challenged me to dream again, tap into my inner Prey Drive to want to build something magical, and have a *Big Ass Exit...*

Jason Mickool is a master who combines a challenger mindset, an impeccable critical-thinking skill set, and an ability to duplicate and replicate a proven system that will do over a billion dollars in the near future.

Anyone who wants to really expand and experience quantum leaps would be an idiot not to dive into this book and see what Mickool is up to at The Greatness Lab (www.greatnesslab.com) as he is replicating his success in round two of what he built in company one.

I think it has a high probability of success, just like the proven system Jason has built.

—Coach Micheal Burt
23X author
Wall Street Journal Best Seller
Founder of The Greatness Factory
Former championship Coach

TABLE OF CONTENTS

INTRODUCTION

Most founders create jobs rather than build true businesses, and even fewer manage to develop platforms. This book provides a sort of cheat code, offering aspiring entrepreneurs opportunities to build substantial businesses phase by phase. While the journey is not easy, it can be straightforward if you have the right mindset and a clear roadmap.

Like many people, my journey began with a strong desire to start a business, fueled by personal circumstances. This desire can stem from being laid off, feeling that your boss doesn't perform as well as you do, dissatisfaction with your career, or even getting passed over for a job. This inner fire ignites a determination to venture out on your own and launch a business, which is an exhilarating place to be.

However, most businesses do not succeed. This book will help you transform that desire into a sustainable fire that leads to building a platform business in the simplest way possible. Typically, most businesses start from a state of chaos, facing limited resources, insufficient funds, and often ambitious yet unconventional ideas aimed at overcoming their current situation.

This book does not focus on how to write a compelling business plan, secure funding, or create an effective pitch deck. Instead, it emphasizes the importance of building something that can grow into something bigger. The concept of a platform suggests that it creates an environment where each person can advance themselves while also contributing to the growth of their business. This approach differs significantly from that of most founders, who often merely replicate a job.

Many founders think they can do a better job than their previous boss and set out to create businesses. However, they frequently find themselves earning less, taking on more responsibilities, and experiencing higher stress levels. Ironically, the activities they initially enjoyed often become overshadowed by tasks they don't find fulfilling. While some founders build successful businesses, many settle for creating jobs for themselves.

You are making a healthy living with some flexibility and opportunity. While you have some staff and infrastructure, very few people reach the next level. This next level refers to today's businesses, which are often larger, such as Apple and Amazon, but there are many examples in between. For instance, an electrician may start a company to provide electrical services. While in St. Petersburg, we have Power Design, a national firm that began here and specializes in commercial electric work.

There is a significant difference between operating as a small business and functioning as a platform. Platforms aren't just about taking on bigger jobs with greater responsibility; they create environments where others can achieve their goals. They build ecosystems where everyone involved has the potential for unlimited success beyond their wildest dreams. As an entrepreneur, your job is to discover the key to unlocking that potential, something most entrepreneurs never find.

When I first started my business, I wanted to be free of dealing with a boss who never truly understood my job or the challenges it presented. However, I soon realized that to build a successful platform, I had to go from having one boss with conflicting priorities to becoming everyone's boss. If not managed correctly, this could limit my freedoms. I found myself responsible for employees, clients, regulators, and family members, all looking to me for direction on how to grow the business.

Finding clarity is a challenging journey. Vision-based leadership, by its very nature, can be disruptive because it lacks a clear path forward; it offers only direction and guidance. This often leads to stress and chaos in your life and in the lives of those around you. Imagine playing Monopoly: you are the banker, the player, the person setting up the board, and even building the plastic houses. You are responsible for printing the money. This encapsulates the essence of entrepreneurship.

Most entrepreneurs start with limited resources and often "fake it until they make it" as they work to establish a sustainable business and gain traction in the marketplace. The goal is to make it appear that you are more substantial than you are, even while you are the only one handling everything.

This book is a cheat code for success. It's not about making things look easy; instead, it offers simple clarity through actionable steps that help you think effectively. The goal is to avoid creating a self-imposed prison: a job with more responsibility, less pay, and no real growth. What you want is to build a business or platform that enables you to achieve your highest potential.

Level One focuses on you. This stage may involve a loved one, a friend, or even a dog as a partner. Level Two is where you start gaining traction, bringing in people who share your vision and come to work every day. During these Level Two years, you are essentially building a ship while sailing it. Everyone around you may want the ship to be finished before setting sail, but that's just not possible; you have to do both simultaneously.

Once you gain traction, you move to Level Three, where you establish systems that replace the need for the best employee or superhero producer. It's about shifting from reliance on one person to relying on a team, thereby removing discretion from operations.

Level Four is the pivotal moment when others start building the business you've created. This is critical mass: when you realize you have a platform, it indicates that others are taking on responsibilities to keep building and growing, which leads to greater achievements.

To give you some context, I started my business after being fired three times and then experiencing a reorganization that left me feeling lost and frustrated. I was unsure about my next steps as a corporate executive.

One day, while my wife and I were out enjoying a strategic afternoon of drinking, I found myself contemplating my future. During that conversation, she bluntly reminded me that I was capable and encouraged me to take a chance on myself. She suggested that we could make this work together, and even if it didn't, we could always start over. That encouragement became the catalyst I needed to pursue what has now become my platform.

Ultimately, what we're discussing is not a new concept; it's about whatever business you choose to pursue. It's something already within you that you know is important and worthwhile and that you believe you can excel at.

It doesn't matter whether you're starting a car shop, a coffee shop, an electrical company, or a landscaping business; the specifics of the venture are not what's important. What truly matters is that you can't sit around and complain about your current job or the opportunities it offers until you take that first step.

To successfully get that first step off the ground, it's not about seeking freedom or getting rich. It's about having a burning desire to create something great. If you approach your venture with the right mindset, one focused on building something magnificent, and you're willing to commit 100 percent to that goal, you're in the right position to create something truly amazing.

So, let's get started. We'll discuss strategy, level up our approach by adding one piece at a time, and outline the steps to build a remarkable platform business.

PHASE

One

*(It's mostly just
you… and maybe your dog.)*

Chapter 1

LEAD YOURSELF FIRST

This opening chapter represents the first phase of our journey. I tend to think of the stages of this phase in a similar way, and I refer to them as the "garage years."

It's interesting: most successful businesses are said to have started in a garage, like Apple or Amazon. However, not everyone begins their journey in a garage. What the term really signifies is that it's just you, possibly with a partner who shares your vision.

In these early stages, it's essential to recognize that the path to success starts with a decision or a dream, a vision of something that has the potential to be extraordinary. The challenge is that no one else may grasp what that dream or vision is, and it can be difficult to articulate what your business will ultimately look like. All you have is this deep-seated desire to make it happen; it's an ambition that you can't detail on a resume. It's a form of greatness that you must define in your mind, often with some guidance or coaching. So, the journey begins with this crucial first step.

It's also important to note that some businesses remain trapped in their "garage years." Many ventures fail because they can't overcome the fundamental challenges of building a strong business foundation. Leading yourself is the first and most critical step. When you achieve success, you'll look back on this part of your journey and have stories to tell about it.

This is similar to when your parents talk about walking to school in the snow without shoes and uphill both ways. You know, those stories about the tough times that people share on their journey to success.

There's no celebration, no team rallying around you. It's just you. That can be hard because the toughest part of leading anyone is often leading yourself.

Motivation can fluctuate, and when frustration sets in, the momentum may not be in your favor. So, what will you do? One of the most important things you need is a routine.

American educator and author Stephen Covey says, "You don't prioritize your schedule; you schedule your priorities." This principle is fundamental. It starts with time management. You need to set up your calendar in a way that positions you for success.

From my observation, most successful people wake up early. If you don't start your day early, no one else will do it for you. You set the tone and pace for what will ultimately define your business and platform.

When you build your calendar and schedule your priorities, they should start at six o'clock in the morning. I've never encountered anyone who said, "I'll start my day at 10:30 and end at five," and then achieved great success. You have to be willing to make sacrifices.

This is crucial because everything ultimately falls on you. Remember, no one is coming to save you. This leads to a key attribute I've noticed in people who find success in life, especially those who become entrepreneurs or build platform businesses: personal responsibility.

Personal responsibility is a vital quality. I once spoke to a friend about a person who used to work for him. I asked what he liked most about her, and after thinking for a moment, he replied, "She is the most personally responsible person I've ever met."

I probed further, asking what he meant by that. He explained, "Without direction, guidance, or being asked to do anything, she consistently delivers at a level that I couldn't even imagine." That's an ideal trait to have in someone you hire or work with.

The question you need to ask yourself is this: *Is this for me?* When I started working from home, my wife teased me. I would get up at six o'clock in the morning to begin my work at what I jokingly called my office, which was really just our kitchen table. By 6:15, I was already working with a cup of coffee. My wife, who at the time had her own job and didn't work for my company, would come down and ask, "What are you doing? It's just you!"

Despite her questions, I filled my days with what would eventually grow into a financial services platform business. No matter how I felt, I showed up every single day, regardless of whether I had something scheduled on my calendar. If I didn't have any appointments, I would create my own. I made sure to include specific tasks and goals so my calendar wasn't just filled with empty time blocks.

I learned early on that having white space in your calendar, meaning time slots with nothing planned, often leads to unproductive time. So, one of the first and most important steps is to fill your calendar every single day. Consistency is key when it comes to business.

Step two is to sell the dream before it even exists. When you're starting a business, you need to have a compelling story or a "value proposition." This not only explains why clients will buy from you but also why potential employees would want to work with you, why vendors would want to partner with you to distribute their products, and why investors would consider funding you in the future.

In the early stages of my business, I didn't have anything tangible to show; all I had was my story. One of the biggest limiting beliefs people have is what I call the "law of the lid." This concept suggests that you can only envision a future based on your current perspective of the world.

It's essential to think ahead five, ten, or even fifteen years and create a vision that is big enough and worthy of your greatest efforts. If you can't communicate that vision to others, they won't believe in your future. So, it's crucial to lay that groundwork as soon as possible so people can truly have faith in your vision and in what you're actually building.

When I started the business, I wanted it to be a business of businesses, almost like a franchise. My business happens to be in the financial services industry.

Many people, even in their business names, use terms like "Capital" or "Wealth Management." When my wife and I were sitting at the table brainstorming names, we lived in Florida. We wanted to create a company of financial advisors, and that was my intent. So, we named ourselves Florida Financial Advisors.

My first group asked me, "Why did you name the place Florida Financial Advisors?"

I replied, "Because I want to build something magnificent and great, something for people like you who come to work here and aspire to become successful financial advisors, and we happen to be in Florida."

A common question people ask is about the five-year vision. I remember discussing our vision with others, saying, "It's so big that this organization will be so vast you won't recognize it when we get there."

Once you have a compelling vision, one of the most critical components that you must carefully consider is your first few hires. These people will help carry the weight to achieve your vision. It's important to view these initial hires not merely as employees; instead, consider giving them titles like "partners," "managing partners," "VPs," or "executives." You want them to feel that the vision is expansive and that they are integral to it.

Allow them to make decisions that align with your organizational vision. These first hires become the DNA of your culture. You define this culture by outlining the behaviors required to execute the vision and by allowing them to embody it.

I always emphasize that those initial hires are crucial; they are the missionaries who will share your story.

They're going to share the story just as you would, helping to multiply it over and over again. I've heard people say, "I don't understand what you're doing. I don't like these products or services, and I don't see how we're going to build this."

I always remind them, "We are building a ship while we are sailing it."

Vision-based leadership can be challenging. It's not just about following processes; it's about having a clear direction, establishing behaviors, and understanding where you are headed. My advice is to be audacious with your vision but also keep your feet on the ground.

I recommend that you approach building a sales organization slowly at first, focusing on the right people. Hire individuals who can convincingly express their desire to embrace your vision, rather than you trying to convince them to buy into it.

While hiring the right people is crucial, it's equally important to address the situation if new hires aren't aligned with your vision. If they demonstrate naysayer tendencies and lack commitment, showing up late, not putting in the effort, you need to let them go quickly. I often say, "Hire slowly, fire fast," if someone isn't a good fit.

In these early stages, you're not just building a company; you're cultivating a culture and establishing a belief system. You are defining expectations and creating behavioral norms to ultimately create culture. As Peter Drucker, the father of modern management, is often credited with saying, *"Culture eats strategy for breakfast."*

There will be times when you doubt yourself. Recognize that you are on the right track when you experience self-doubt, as it indicates opportunities for improvement. You'll feel frustrated that progress isn't as swift as you'd like, and you may even question your life choices. Expect to work long hours, from six in the morning until eight at night. You'll find yourself doing payroll while others enjoy leisure time at the beach.

On our honeymoon, my wife was solely responsible for payroll one day because our employees needed to be paid. It was a whole day spent working during what was supposed to be a special time for us.

It's normal to experience frustration, burnout, poor decision-making regarding employees, and issues with vision and time management. These feelings can be overwhelming at times. However, one thing you must never do is give up.

By focusing on your goals and managing your time effectively, breaking things down quarter by quarter, month by month, week by week, and day by day, you will ultimately build a successful business.

Sales should be the top priority. In the early years of a business, many people make poor decisions because they focus on aspects that don't directly contribute to the most important goal: generating sales and revenue.

One common mistake is becoming preoccupied with the details of where the office will be located, how it will look, and what furniture will be necessary. While these things can create a sense of accomplishment and make it feel like you're making progress, they do not drive revenue for the business.

Instead, dedicate your time and energy to identifying your next customer. Consider your branding strategies and how you will convert potential clients. Focus on tracking your conversion rates so that acquiring subsequent clients becomes easier than landing the first one.

Avoid spending time on tasks like scouting real estate or purchasing desks, furniture, and printers. In today's world, you can effectively work from home. Many tools, like Zoom, help you keep your expenses low. If you prioritize driving revenue while keeping your expenses manageable, you'll be better equipped to navigate the challenging first two years of building a business, which are often the toughest.

Real entrepreneurs should focus on sales, activity, and lead conversion. Once the formula for acquiring a client is established in terms of cost and activity time, you begin packaging the sales process and training others to do it. That is the key to scaling.

What I've found is that several factors can keep people from making good decisions.

First, many people are looking for shortcuts. They attempt to outsource client acquisition or revenue-generating activities to third parties, which rarely works because it's not a replicable system that can be easily transferred to others.

Second, some people misuse the freedom in their calendars by prioritizing personal activities over their business. For example, they might plan to go to the gym at 10:00 a.m. and then expect to return and work afterward, but they often struggle with effective time management.

The third issue is also related to time management. When people have gaps in their calendars, they may fill them randomly rather than focusing on structured goals and targets in their weekly plans. They might fail to set clear objectives for each week that they aim to achieve.

Lastly, many people seek advice and coaching from individuals who aren't equipped to provide the right guidance. Coaching can significantly influence a businessperson's success, so it's essential to seek input from those who are more successful or have accomplished what you want to achieve.

It's crucial to avoid taking advice from people who do not have the business that you aspire to create, even if their business is successful but doesn't align with your goals. For instance, if I have a conversation with a friend who owns an event planning business, she may be passionate about her work, but she is essentially the business. When she asks me how to scale her business and struggles to comprehend my answers, instead of seeking to understand the complexities, she might just dismiss them.

Be cautious about the advice you take and ensure that you regularly seek coaching from those who truly want to see you thrive, not just those who want to avoid seeing you in pain or struggle. Connect with people who have built the business you wish to create in the future.

Analysis paralysis is a common challenge that many people face. They often attempt to build the entire system before engaging with clients. Instead of focusing on providing value to their clients and prospects, they get caught up in creating the perfect brochure or website or in managing their Google local listings.

What they should prioritize is meeting as many clients and prospects as possible to understand their needs and preferences, as it will help them identify what products or services people are willing to buy.

Chapter 2

SELLING THE DREAM BEFORE IT EXISTS

One of the most important things for any business to understand is that it doesn't matter whether you are manufacturing a product or providing a service. What truly matters is your ability to deliver and sell effectively. When building a company, the specifics of what you are creating are less important than attracting clients, employees, and other stakeholders to your vision. Therefore, it's crucial to communicate this dream to everyone involved, early and often.

Ask yourself: *Who are we? What do we truly stand for? What kind of company are we building? What makes us unique? What is our value proposition?* Even if your value proposition is similar to that of a competitor, it's essential to articulate and market it properly.

Consider why you started the business. What's the story behind it? In the beginning, you may lack credibility, but the most significant asset you have is your understanding of the problem you're trying to solve for the consumer. This understanding is critical. Reflect on the experiences that led you to this business and equipped you to address that problem.

Additionally, your leadership is vital. Whether dealing with clients, employees, or vendors, everyone wants to know what your goals are. They want to understand where you are heading, which is ultimately about the vision you have for the organization.

It is your responsibility to articulate and deliver the value proposition of your business. What people are truly buying into is a belief system, not just in your products or services but in you and your vision. Therefore, you must provide opportunities for growth when hiring new members.

When bringing people onto your team, I always prioritize eagerness over readiness. What does this mean? Many entrepreneurs, especially when starting out, struggle to convey their vision and often evaluate potential hires through a lens of skepticism. They tend to focus on the negative aspects of a person's abilities rather than considering their potential.

To effectively sell your vision, you must give people the chance to participate in it as equals. Instead of thinking, *I wish this person could do this, but they lack certain skills*, you should look for those moments when your first hire shows promise, like arriving early, staying late, making extra phone calls, or following up diligently.

When you notice these traits, tap that person on the shoulder and say, "I see something special in you that I believe will make you a key contributor to this organization in the future." Encourage that person by assigning them meaningful tasks to prove themselves, with the promise of promotion. You will find that people often rise to the occasion, but it's crucial that you, as the leader, prioritize these moments.

If you can't communicate your vision effectively, it doesn't matter how great your business is. We frequently ask ourselves: *Who are we? What makes us unique? Why did we start this business? Where are we headed?*

Selling an early belief in your vision gives your business its first heartbeat. This initial engagement shapes the clarity and direction of your organization for every consumer, employee, and partner. Remember, while your first five employees may join for money, they are motivated by more than just financial compensation. We refer to this as "money, marbles, and chalk."

While people will work for money, they are equally motivated by intangibles, like recognition and the opportunity for personal growth, especially in today's social media landscape. They join because of your excitement and vision, not solely for monetary benefits.

No one is ever completely ready for the job they are about to take on. Instead, they are ready for the opportunities you create. You have the power to design what those opportunities look like on a day-to-day basis. It's essential to articulate the activities required and provide training while simultaneously promoting the potential future of the business.

As the founder, you must transfer your belief in this vision until the reality catches up. Engage everyone in the vision daily, from the recruitment process to onboarding clients, ensuring that everyone contributes to the growth of the business.

One of the key factors driving our success is our mission statement. It's essential to have a compelling vision that outlines where we are, where we're going, and why we aim to get there. Equally important is understanding what our company truly stands for.

Many companies struggle because they create missions that are too focused on clients and not enough on people. Our mission is to elevate people to the highest possible level in their careers and lives. When we say "people," we mean more than just our clients; it includes every staff member, employee, salesperson, and anyone we interact with, including communities and charitable organizations. Our ultimate goal is to help everyone reach their full potential.

We want every person we hire to strive for personal improvement, subscribing to the idea that there is no end to "better." We are looking for people who, when they look in the mirror each morning, say to themselves, *I want to become a better person.* By contrast, we want to avoid hiring those who are simply seeking a job rather than a career.

It's not just about filling a position; it's about finding people who are passionate about their growth. When your team buys into this mission, it has a transformative effect; they begin to believe in themselves and trust that the company has their best interests at heart. This belief is what helps create a strong, positive company culture and work environment.

One of the things we should discuss is eagerness and how to create it. Eagerness comes from having self-confidence and a strong belief system about oneself, which most people do not possess.

According to Shad Helmsetter, author of *What to Say When You Talk to Yourself,* "*Research shows that eighty percent of what we say to ourselves is not particularly positive.*" This starts to change when someone begins to believe in us. When others recognize our positive behaviors, even the smallest sparks, it can ignite a sense of eagerness within us. People tend to seek out more of that positive reinforcement, which, in turn, reduces the negative self-talk.

For instance, if I recognize a talent in someone, no matter how small, I let them know. For example, I might say, "Hey, I see something special in you; you always come in early and stay late." Even if that wasn't their usual behavior, suddenly that person adopts the label of "the early bird" or "the dedicated employee." This recognition helps to foster eagerness.

It's essential to embrace a model where mastery comes from being a student, a practitioner, and eventually a teacher. By nurturing the skills of practitioners, we can create eagerness. Every person should strive to become the best version of themselves, especially when the overarching mission is to elevate people to the highest possible level in their careers and lives.

By consistently providing direct feedback and encouraging people to train others, you create the student-practitioner-teacher cycle and help them become experts. This can transform the business, as everyone desires to become proficient and share their knowledge.

In college, I took a Pascal programming class, and it was one of the most difficult I had ever taken. I was failing miserably. I reached the add/drop deadline and was going to give up, as I didn't think I had the mind for it. I didn't think I would be able to figure it out, no matter how much time I had.

A good friend of mine had a different vision for me. He said, "Don't give up. Map it out." He committed to learning the programming language with me: he worked with me to build a schedule, held me accountable, was there when I was stuck, and would come to the lab and help answer questions, as it came naturally to him. He helped manage my negative thoughts when I was frustrated, and most importantly, he took the time to explain concepts. It was his belief and conviction, along with his time, that led me to get an A in the class.

As a leader, you must create an environment of eagerness and growth, which may require taking some hits along the way. Your support can help others become the leaders they need to be to execute your mission and vision effectively.

The question is, how do you navigate through challenging times?

To answer that, let's first consider another question: Do you know why the British wore red in the American Revolution?

The answer is that it was meant to address the psychological impact of bleeding. The British found that if soldiers saw their comrades bleeding or scared, it could create a ripple effect of fear among the troops.

One of the challenges you may face is when your vision and results aren't aligned. During such times, people will look to you to maintain faith in the mission and vision of the business. As a leader, it's crucial never to let your team see you bleed or sweat.

If you have a solid vision and a good system in place, everything will eventually work out as long as you stay focused on sales. However, you can't control how long it will take or the ups and downs you will experience. During these fluctuations, if you don't keep your team moving in the right direction, your vision could be derailed. They may lose faith in your ability to execute.

So, you need to stay resilient. Even when things don't seem to be going right, maintain a positive attitude and continue developing your people. Engage key team members, involve them in the mission, and regularly ask for their input. For example, present results and then ask, "What suggestions do you have?" "What would you do if this were your business?" "What would be the key things you would do to get us back on track?"

To keep the momentum going, you need to create positive incentives and celebrate small successes. In our culture, we do things like setting a monthly leaderboard to highlight the best of the best and ad hoc lunches for small victories. We refer to these types of incentives as "money, marbles, and chalk." In business, this is a framework to think about how you create and use incentives. "Marbles" are the visible rewards—trophies and awards that you can put on the shelf as a reminder of your success in periods of time, the quick hits of validation that feel good. "Chalk" is the scoreboard—metrics, rankings, and performance tracking that show whether you're improving and moving forward. "Money" is the obvious one, but it doesn't have to be large; it could also be trips or gift cards, big and small, to go with the other two. But the recognition that truly matters isn't about money or status. It's about being seen. It's about someone acknowledging your effort, your growth, your discipline, and your progress—especially when the results aren't yet fully visible. Real leaders understand that people don't just want compensation; they want confirmation that their work, commitment, and development matter.

Transparency is not a sign of weakness as long as it is paired with positivity. Act on the feedback from your team and turn their suggestions into actionable plans and initiatives that will guide you back to your goals.

Chapter 3

MAKE YOUR FIRST
FIVE HIRES COUNT

Making your first hires count is arguably one of the most important components for scaling and moving your business beyond its early stages. This process is essential for setting the foundation.

First and foremost, early hires significantly influence company culture. As I mentioned before, culture eats strategy for breakfast, so it's vital to define the behaviors and norms that will guide your team. Clear expectations help employees understand when they are aligned with the culture and when they are not.

Another crucial consideration when making your first hire is whether you're building a business or a platform. If you're building a platform, your goal from day one is to replicate yourself. That means you need to hire people who can help you grow and scale your business effectively.

To provide some context, my first hire was a recruiter named Hans Pierre. When we started the business, my intent was not to become a financial advisor, although I have many successful friends in that field. Instead, I wanted to operate as an executive in a financial services firm, creating a business of businesses, specifically, a business of financial advisors.

I remember the process of hiring Hans. I posted a job on Indeed, interviewed him online, and, interestingly, never met him in person before hiring him. After almost a year of working with us, he told me that his parents thought I had been trying to smuggle him. I had flown him to Chicago under a company name that didn't even exist at the time, operated by an LLC that hadn't been established.

He showed up in a Patriots hoodie, with messy hair and an unshaven face, and didn't really understand what he was getting into, but I hired him anyway. He had no prior experience, but he excelled at taking direction, which was exactly what I needed. I needed someone who could handle tasks.

So, what did he do? He posted job openings and set up interviews.

He became the heartbeat of our operations and my first ambassador, consistently communicating my vision. He could articulate what I was thinking, which ultimately translated into PowerPoint presentations. Together, we cultivated a team of individuals who embodied a belief system based on discipline rather than just resumes.

We would ask questions like, "Why you? This is our mission; where do you think you would fit in?" We discussed the leadership path we were creating and asked candidates if they had ever thought about taking on a leadership role and what they envisioned for themselves. We prioritized character over credentials.

When you hire people with the right character who genuinely buy into your vision, you're not just looking for someone who fits a specific role. The right person is one who can be coached into the culture you aspire to create: hardworking, successful people with the right daily habits.

After hiring someone, the first step is to provide them with a roadmap. You set the tone and pace as the leader.

Train the necessary habits from the start. Everyone should be in by 7:30 a.m.; this is non-negotiable. It's essential because every success story begins with, "I started early and left late." If you want to be successful, arriving early and staying late should be the expectation.

Time management is crucial. Everything must be scheduled, even personal activities like going to the gym. You have to teach people organizational skills. In my experience, a lack of time management and organizational skills leads to missed tasks and incomplete work.

Here's a basic tip: when an email arrives, respond to it and then file it away. I've learned over the years that those who don't organize or filter their emails, or those who let them pile up, often fail to follow up and don't finish what they started.

You need to establish clear norms from day one. Cultural norms have been part of corporate America for many years, focusing not just on results but also on behaviors. I learned from a woman named Teresa Hanratty, the youngest senior vice president of one of the largest financial service firms in the country, that norms can serve as operating guidelines for the behaviors everyone on the leadership team should follow. Personally, this concept evolved into identifying behaviors that frustrate me.

I believe that norms truly take root in a culture when everyone has the opportunity to contribute to defining them. In the early days, we would establish our norms and then ask the team, "Is there anything that frustrates you about our behaviors, yours or those of others, that we could work on together?"

We started revisiting these norms quarterly and ranking ourselves on a scale of one to ten based on our adherence to them. This process encouraged self-reflection: we would ask ourselves whether we were living in alignment with these norms or straying from them.

Some of the norms we discussed included:

- Be present
- Stay engaged
- Seek 70 percent agreement, 100 percent support
- Defend those who are absent
- Communicate concerns

If there's no clarity about what is expected, people may act however they choose, which can harm your culture. Let me give you some examples. One such norm is "Lombardi time."

I introduced Lombardi time because I find it frustrating when people arrive late to meetings, even by a few minutes. If a meeting starts at 7:30 a.m., I want everyone there by that time. Lombardi time means that if you arrive on time, you're actually late. I encourage everyone to show up five minutes early to avoid the risk of being late.

Another important norm is "be present." In today's environment, there are many distractions, like social media (Snapchat, Instagram, etc.) and emails. In meetings or training sessions, I noticed people often turned off their cameras during Zoom calls, scrolled through their phones, or checked their emails whenever they heard a notification.

The "be present" norm emphasizes that no multitasking is allowed. It encourages everyone to stay focused and present during meetings and training. If someone is distracted by their phone or email, we can address it without taking it personally.

Additionally, we have the "defend the absent" norm. There are often instances in any culture when one person will complain about another. They may approach a supervisor or leader to say that someone isn't doing their job properly. This behavior can create silos and disrupt relationships within the organization, leading to a negative culture.

The "defend the absent" norm states that if someone comes to you with complaints about another person, you cannot engage in that negativity. Instead, you have a responsibility to bring those individuals together to challenge any assumptions about someone's laziness or lack of commitment. This is one of the most important norms you can instill in an organization to encourage everyone to work together through consensus and maintain strong relationships.

One thing that always drove me crazy was people's attire: things like not having collar stays, wearing unshined shoes, not wearing a tie, having an unironed shirt, or neglecting haircuts and eyebrows. One of the norms we have is: "Dress for the job you want, not the one you have."

This sets a standard of professionalism among team members. If someone is dressed poorly, I can say to them, "Dress for the job you want, not the one you have. What norm are you violating today?"

Next is "state what you're for," which centers on consensus and the ability to move forward. When making group-based decisions, especially when hiring the first five employees to shape the culture and environment and pursue the company vision, there will always be numerous challenges. I've heard talk of having "ninety-nine problems" or "seventy-five problems." What I know is that in building any organization, there will always be room for improvement.

Often, the reason these issues remain unaddressed is that there is always a competing priority and an endless list of problems to tackle. "State what you're for" is a reminder during meetings in which we are making decisions related to our vision: if someone is complaining, we need to focus on "state what you're for." If they have a solution, we can move forward. If they're just voicing a complaint without offering a solution, then they're violating a norm.

Another critical aspect of consensus is the idea of "70 percent agreement, 100 percent support." Even if I don't fully agree with your point of view, I need to reach at least 70 percent agreement. In board meetings, particularly in smaller companies, decisions are often made by the leader, and if someone disagrees, they might undermine that decision through their actions or behavior.

This norm allows us to assess the extent of disagreement: Do you disagree by 50 percent, 40 percent, or is your stance a complete zero? If we can establish a compromise that achieves at least 70 percent agreement, we can move forward effectively.

Lastly, there's the tough reminder: "No one cares about you." My boss used to say this whenever I raised concerns by saying, "I don't like this because it affects me." He would remind me that, in the grand scheme of things, no one cares about personal issues; the focus should be on the mission. Many people feel upset when I state, "Nobody cares about you," but it serves as a reality check to help prioritize company goals over individual initiatives or personal egos and agendas.

When you embrace a mindset of servitude, where the focus is on others rather than yourself, you can create a positive culture within your organization. This allows everyone to feel good about the community you've built while working toward your mission and vision.

It's important to ask questions rather than just answer inquiries about yourself. Engage others by seeking their thoughts and experiences. When someone expresses uncertainty, often the first question we ask is, "Have you read the material?" We then encourage them to read it again and ensure they are prepared to seek the necessary support.

This approach helps train individuals to become more self-sufficient. By hiring the right salespeople and recruiters who align with our mission, we instilled our vision in our first five hires. This foundational culture set a standard for the business's future growth.

My goal was never to find clients for myself; instead, I aimed to equip others with leads, scripts, training, and opportunities. By doing this, I allowed them to seek clients for their businesses. Our focus was on helping them build their own enterprises and execute our mission: to elevate people to the highest possible level in their careers and lives.

Another crucial norm we established was that our relationships could not be fragile. I found this particularly important because there were times when, as a leader, I would unintentionally say things that upset someone. In some cases, people left the team without sharing their reasons, only to later discover the impact of those comments.

It's essential that relationships do not become fragile, so we established a norm that they should be resilient. If I say something inappropriate or have a bad day that affects my behavior, it's important that we both recognize that our relationship must withstand these moments. You need to feel empowered to give me feedback, and I need to be able to accept it.

Conversely, we must have a strong enough relationship for me to give feedback and for you to accept it. The reason that is so important is that my perception is my reality. For our relationships not to be fragile and for us to stay focused on the organization's mission, we must be able to give and receive feedback to and from one another.

I want to be able to make mistakes while still maintaining your respect, regardless of any specific situation. We must separate our personalities from our work to achieve the best possible outcomes and effectively collaborate toward our mission and vision.

One key norm is that leadership starts from the front. Often, as people advance in their careers, they may adopt a "do as I say, not as I do" mentality. In my experience at other organizations, senior leadership often disengaged from training sessions, feeling they were above participation; they would be preoccupied with checking emails in the back of the room while expecting everyone else to engage fully.

Leading from the front means being a role model who inspires others. Every leader must actively participate, demonstrating through their actions—showing, telling, and doing—not just delegating tasks. This includes being present, arriving early, staying late, and taking risks.

Another crucial norm is that each team member is responsible for their own development. People often express feelings of stagnation or a lack of guidance, but I've come to realize that personal development is ultimately the responsibility of the individual, not just the leader. Therefore, it is essential for each person to create their own individual development plan, outlining the skills and behaviors they wish to improve, along with specific actions they will take.

Trusting the process is vital, especially when doubts arise about the sales process, product, or any other elements of our work. The norm of "trust the process" encourages team members to seek understanding before jumping to conclusions or making negative judgments. It's important to grasp why certain decisions were made and clearly define the desired outcomes.

From a management perspective, when making the first five hires, it's crucial to help everyone involved in the decision-making process understand that it cannot be about their preferences alone. There will be times when leadership decisions may be unfavorable to an individual but are nonetheless the right course of action for the company's success.

To effectively manage an organization, it's essential to adopt a manager's perspective rather than just that of an advisor or staff member. We call this MPOV, "manager's point of view." This means having the perspective of a board of directors rather than a manager of tasks, thinking about how things affect the larger initiative and the values of the company.

The concept of "everything's always excellent" revolves around maintaining a positive atmosphere within the organization. This idea was inspired by a scene in the movie *Saving Private Ryan*.

In this scene, Tom Hanks, as the character leading the group, is confronted by Matt Damon, who expresses surprise that Hanks never seems to complain. Hanks clarifies that while he does voice his frustrations, he vents upwards to his superiors because they are the ones who can help him solve problems. This emphasizes the principle of "everything's always excellent": when someone is negative in the workplace, it's important to address their behavior directly and remind them of the organization's values.

Understand that when you are building cultures of good behavior, there will always be people who are going to try to undermine what you're trying to build. We've all worked with people whose bad attitude ruins the day; these people tend to find recruits. The following is not the norm; rather, it is something to watch out for. Misery loves company; there will always be some people in any organization who resist their tasks. They may seek out others to share their distractions, discussing everything from sports to social events, which can detract from productivity.

Respecting your workplace is crucial, especially in a startup environment. People may feel at ease leaving their dishes in the sink or neglecting to clean out the refrigerator. This can be frustrating for others who struggle to deal with clutter or unpleasantness in shared spaces. It's important to focus on addressing behaviors rather than attacking individuals, fostering a culture of accountability.

The phrase "I am the problem; I am the solution" highlights the importance of personal responsibility. If you are not holding yourself accountable for the challenges you face, you might find it difficult to move forward effectively. When you reach a place in your life where you realize you are the problem and the solution to everything, it's liberating because you take responsibility, and no one can control your results or attitude. Your success will reach new heights.

Your value in the marketplace is determined by how others perceive your offerings. If sales are low or conversions aren't meeting expectations, it's not necessarily a flaw in your script, leadership, leads, or training. The marketplace decides your value, and you must be willing to adjust your approach accordingly.

Remember the old adage: "When the going gets tough, the tough get going." It emphasizes resilience and the need to adapt in challenging times. Never give up, because giving up is what determines whether you succeed or fail. If you understand that the journey ahead is going to be tough, remember that trouble is not in the way; it's on the way. You can't allow trouble to obstruct your path.

"Read it, read it again, and read it one more time" means solving your own problems before asking for help. It's about creating a culture of self-reliance rather than asking people questions before you have actually tried to solve problems on your own. Read it, reflect on it, and ask more questions.

In interactions with others, prioritize effectiveness over being right. Often, you may find yourself in a debate. Ask yourself: *What do I want the outcome to be? What do I hope to gain from this situation?* Most of the time, especially when you are in a leadership role or trying to influence others, your goal isn't simply to be right; it's to get the job done.

"Fly the plane" is a principle for managing crises within an organization. The primary reason a plane crashes during a crisis is that the pilot loses focus. We studied a leader who was a former military pilot, analyzing transcripts from various plane crashes. In every incident, the cause was human error. The critical rule during an emergency, especially during takeoff and landing, is to climb to thirty thousand feet and wait for guidance.

Often, when a crisis arises and alarms start ringing, people become distracted by them and lose sight of what is essential. For example, JFK Jr. tragically flew into the water because he didn't "fly the plane." In business, to "fly the plane" means that, regardless of the challenges you face, you still need to serve clients and generate sales. It doesn't matter if the computer system is down or the phone system isn't working; you must remain focused on getting the job done.

As your team gets busier, you may notice a decline in the quality of work. This can be troubling. If your name is attached to a project, it must be excellent. Achieving excellence requires both quality and quantity.

The concept of "volunteering for everything" emerged as teams grew and moved beyond the early startup phase. In meetings, when projects or initiatives were discussed, people often hesitated to raise their hands. Instead of shying away, we aimed to encourage those who were willing to embrace new challenges and contribute to improving the business. "Volunteering for everything" was introduced to fan the flames of enthusiasm and collaboration.

"No entitlement" means that people are entitled to nothing beyond an opportunity. For instance, if there's no coffee in the coffee pot, so what? There is no entitlement in this organization. If someone else has the best leads, again, so what? There is no entitlement here; go out and generate your own. It's essential that people understand this. Your role is to address any misbehavior by using established norms to help change it.

Is it possible to determine someone's potential success in our culture through an interview? Over the years, I've learned that it's not always effective. I used to hire Division I athletes or magna cum laude graduates with great personalities and communication skills. I thought, *This person is incredible; they will be wildly successful here.* However, I soon discovered that some of them were lazy, resistant to direction and feedback, consistently late, and often violated the norms of our organization's culture.

Conversely, I've interviewed candidates who left me wondering why they hadn't shaved for the interview, dressed nicer, or demonstrated strong communication skills. I questioned why they were on their third job out of college or why they kept leaving jobs after just one or two years. In those moments, I might have thought they lacked potential. Yet, I was surprised to find that some of them had the heart of a lion and an intense desire to succeed in an organization; they just hadn't found the right opportunity before.

These candidates often became the hardest-working, most professional, and most committed individuals, responsible team members who truly excelled. What I've learned is that you can't always gauge whether someone will be a good fit or have the right qualities just from their resume, and often not even by their answers during an interview.

Instead, it's essential to assess their desire to be part of something that aligns with your mission and values. What we do is conduct a "career preview." Before an interview, candidates go through an overview of our company, its history, culture, mission, vision, values, and how we serve our clients in the financial services sector or whatever industry we're in. We provide them with a strong understanding of who we are.

We encourage them to take notes and conduct research to prepare for the interview. During the interview, we ask questions like, "What did you like about our vision?" "What resonated with you regarding our mission?" "Why do you think you'd be a good fit?" and "How do you see yourself playing a role in what we do?"

Based on their responses, we make our hiring decisions. It's not solely about their resume; it's more about their genuine desire to be part of something special.

When you hire people with a strong desire to be part of something special, they genuinely believe in your mission, vision, values, and the growth trajectory of your organization. These are the candidates you want to hire because they enthusiastically express why they want to be a part of your team.

Every office has its own set of norms that address the specific challenges it faces, especially now that we operate as a platform. Initially, we had one mission, one vision, and one set of values. Today, we still uphold that singular mission, vision, and set of values for the entire company. However, each organization, office, and team can establish its own vision, values, and norms.

One important norm I didn't mention is to "praise in public and punish in private." This principle guides how we provide feedback when someone violates a norm. It means you should never call someone out in front of a large group or publicly reprimand them. Instead, approach the person privately and use a model we teach called "positive, interesting, even better."

For example, you might say, "Hey, you have many great skills; you're a leader among leaders, and you perform well on the phone with good production. However, I've noticed that you seem to struggle to adhere to Lombardi time, often arriving three to five minutes late, or even fifteen minutes late on occasion. What support do you need from us? This is important because it's a norm that reflects our organizational culture, and other team members have begun to notice and comment on this. It can hinder your growth and reputation as a major player in this organization. So, how can I help you avoid violating the norm of Lombardi time?"

Have these discussions behind closed doors to maintain a respectful, constructive environment.

PHASE

Two

*(The hustle breaks if you
don't start building systems.)*

Chapter 4

TRAINING IS LEADERSHIP

Today, we are starting what can be called phase two of our project. Or I like to think of it as building a ship while sailing it; either can describe our current situation.

To break this down, it's crucial to understand what we're starting with. This phase relates to years two through five of a business's growth. I view this training as focused on leadership. When you start a business and begin hiring people, a major challenge you'll face is the tendency to repeat yourself like a broken record.

If you find yourself constantly repeating the same things, it's time to reconsider your training approach and how you will develop your team. The goal is to empower your employees to communicate those key messages themselves.

One of the biggest mistakes I've seen leaders make when trying to scale their businesses is focusing too much on hiring the right people. When this mindset sets in, frustration often arises because finding the right person can feel like searching for a needle in a haystack. Ultimately, the employees you hire reflect the leadership you provide.

Hiring effectively requires a strong leadership style that recognizes there is no such thing as a bad hire. Rather than labeling someone as a bad hire, reflect on what can be done to better equip that person from day one, enabling them to perform at the expected levels without you having to repeat yourself endlessly.

In many instances, when it comes to scaling and growing a business, the issue isn't with the people; it's more about the leadership and systems in place to support them. It's never just about the person you hired. The real issue is usually a systematic problem, indicating that the leadership isn't providing guidance in the right way to help the business grow.

There are no bad hires; there is only ineffective leadership. You'll recognize this when the success of your employees relies on the training systems you've established, rather than on their degrees or job experience.

If you have the right systems in place, and I'll discuss some of the basic systems, you'll be able to develop what we call the "Five Levels of Leadership." Effective leadership is fundamentally about training, whether you're teaching someone to fit a peg into a hole or to deliver a product or service. The key differentiator between great businesses and average ones is how effectively they develop leaders and create systems to support that development.

Shift your focus from doing the job yourself to training others to do it. If you're the founder handling accounting, marketing, sales, manufacturing, and distribution, you must change how you allocate your time and energy to scale your business. The initial shift occurs when you invest your efforts in what Stephen Covey calls "Quadrant II thinking."

This involves time allocation. Instead of spending your time on tasks you enjoy or can do yourself, dedicate it to training others, minimizing your direct involvement.

This transition can be challenging. Rather than doing things solo or one-on-one, tackle tasks in a group setting. Encourage collaboration by asking your team how to improve processes and formalize them so that you can "build a ship and sail it at the same time." Then delegate those tasks to others.

For this approach to be effective, you must master five skills related to developing solid systems in your business. The first skill involves conducting one-on-one meetings. This practice is the cornerstone of growth and essential for establishing a system. In these meetings, the ownership of identifying and solving problems lies with the participant, not the leader facilitating the discussion.

Here are a few essential tips for conducting effective one-on-one meetings:

Over the years, I have conducted many of these meetings. For example, when I met with Sarah, we would set aside half an hour to talk. However, I would typically walk into those meetings unprepared, and Sarah would often be unprepared as well. When I would ask her, "What do you want to talk about?" she would reply, "Geez, I don't know."

As a result, I would end up looking at data and numbers, pointing out the problems I observed. Then I would suggest action items for Sarah to address those issues. I can tell you that this is one of the most frustrating situations for any leader trying to scale a business.

An effective way to run one-on-ones is to focus on key performance indicators (KPIs). In this example, Sarah should prepare a document each week that outlines her targets, whether she met them, the reasons she may not have, and what commitments she will make to succeed over the next seven days.

Once Sarah completes that document, there may be instances when she does not recognize all the areas for improvement.

This is where a feedback loop comes into play. One of the biggest challenges in leading is that people respond differently to feedback. Some appreciate feedback and see it as a gift that helps them grow, while others may view it as criticism.

It's essential to cultivate a culture around the five leadership skills, including mastering the ability to give feedback that is perceived not as criticism but as an opportunity for growth.

The third skill is delegation of commitment. A key principle in leadership is helping people honor and develop their commitments. Instead of dictating what tasks they should complete, encourage them to propose their own ideas regarding their commitments.

The fourth skill is performance coaching. This involves ensuring everyone understands their targets and what they need to achieve each day. In the example above, the responsibility for performance lies with Sarah, not me, the founder or owner. If her targets are not met, it's important that I take action based on the data, provide regular, ongoing feedback to help her course correct, and, in collaboration with her, define commitments to improve performance.

Finally, the most critical aspect is leadership development. Many leaders fail to recognize the desire of people to improve daily. The best way to foster this is by continuously asking them, "Where are you in the process of becoming a manager? Where are you in the process of becoming a VP? What steps are you taking to reach the next level?" Also, ask them about the personal goals they are working on, referred to as "WDYWFY," which encompasses "What do you want for yourself?"

A crucial aspect of this is ensuring that the document outlining the employee's targets is completed before the meeting. This form isn't just about numbers and data; it should also include the person's personal mission statement, business targets, and development goals. What do they need to do every day to achieve their objectives? Also, what are their personal goals?

They should consider what drives them: Do they want to buy a house? Get married? Save for a new car, a boat, or a vacation? All these aspirations should be part of your one-on-one discussion. When the person meets their targets and grows professionally, they also move closer to achieving their personal mission.

Regarding time management, remember this: you can't prioritize your schedule; you must schedule your priorities. This concept comes from Stephen Covey. As part of effective time management, you should block out time in your calendar for personal development. For instance, Google has designated periods during which employees can work on anything they choose, including personal development plans.

Leaders who understand their mission to elevate their team members to their highest potential in both their careers and lives foster an environment that promotes personal development. Regularly ask team members what steps they will take to learn new skills. Ultimately, this philosophy cultivates a culture where the business operates smoothly.

One important concept is the "Five Levels of Leadership." Many frameworks exist for these levels, but the one I want to discuss is inspired by my good friend Ray Kelly. Think about this as I explain it: your mission is to cultivate a team of Level Four leaders.

Let's begin with Level One. A Level One individual can perform their job effectively. At this level, you can assign a task to them and expect it to be done. Without any interaction or questions from you—no "Do you have a second?" or "How would you approach this?"—they can simply do the job. We appreciate Level One individuals for this reason.

It's important that tasks are completed, deadlines are met, and the job is done. Level Two individuals can not only perform their tasks but also identify problems. We value Level Two people as well.

For example, someone might say, "I'm working on this job, and I've encountered a problem." They articulate the issue to you for assistance. They come to you with the challenge they've identified as a bottleneck within their process, system, or organization.

Now let's talk about Level Three individuals. In addition to doing the job and identifying problems, they can also fix those problems consistently without your assistance. We truly appreciate Level Threes.

Why? Level Threes help build freedom in your business. Your organization no longer functions as a job that requires you to solve every issue; you begin to create a team capable of resolving problems on its own. This is where things become really exciting.

Level Four leaders can do everything mentioned: perform the job, identify problems, and fix those problems. However, what sets Level Fours apart is their ability to gather a group of people around a task to consistently solve problems. They are tied back to the company's vision and values.

Just think about it: if you had a team of Level Four leaders, people who could independently do the job, identify issues, fix them, and mobilize others to resolve them continually while aligning with the organization's mission and values, how incredible would that be?

Consider this at any stage of your business. Imagine having a leadership development factory that could consistently produce Level Four leaders!

Then there's Level Five; these leaders can perform the job, identify problems, and so much more. They have the ability to rally people and mobilize a group around a common task to address issues within a situation. However, their primary responsibility, which ties back to the mission, vision, and values of the organization, is to create Level Four leaders.

Doing this involves developing a shared language about what leadership at this level looks like, promoting it, identifying potential leaders, and helping them build plans to become Level Four leaders. Most importantly, their role is to nurture the development of Level Four leaders.

In my experience presenting this material, I have found that people commonly ask two questions. I challenge you to consider them: First, "What level am I?" Second, "How many Level Four leaders do I currently have in my organization?"

Often, when I ask people these questions, they tend to self-identify as being better leaders than they really are. No one wants to perceive themselves as anything less than a Level Four or Five leader.

I recall being in a meeting where I turned to the person next to me and asked, "What level do you think you are?"

He confidently replied, "I'm a Level Four."

I couldn't help but laugh. "You're not a Level Four."

Surprised, he asked, "What do you mean I'm not a Level Four?"

"Let's talk about it after the meeting," I said.

Afterward, Paul approached me, eager to know why I thought he wasn't a Level Four leader. I explained, "You haven't consistently rallied others to solve problems that would yield better results."

At that point, he began to make excuses. He said, "It's not me; it's the market... it's this person... it's the circumstances," and so on.

I interrupted him, saying, "The reality is, you can't be a Level Four leader if you're making excuses for not achieving your targets. Level Four and Level Five leaders don't do that. All you've demonstrated is that you can identify problems, but you can't resolve them because you're focused on excuses."

Needless to say, he no longer works for the company.

This highlights the importance of regularly discussing leadership levels and role expectations. It's crucial to present this framework to your leadership team and ask them to evaluate whether their actions reflect Level One, Two, Three, Four, or Five leadership. If you disagree with their self-assessment, it's essential to provide coaching and feedback on what each level entails.

To establish a thriving leadership culture within an organization, it's essential to start right from the interview process. When we meet potential candidates, we outline what success looks like in our organization by presenting clear career paths.

We have defined levels that correspond to roles like associate manager, district manager, associate vice president, field vice president, regional vice president, senior vice president, or franchise owner. During the interview process, we ask candidates about their career aspirations and where they see themselves in five years. We also encourage them to share any previous leadership positions they've held or their ambitions for growth within our company. This approach helps to embed a leadership-oriented mindset in our culture from the very beginning.

As the organization grows, developing leaders early is crucial, particularly concerning what we call the "span of control." This concept refers to how many people or processes an individual can effectively manage at once. As we add team members, it's vital to create different roles to ensure continued support for organizational growth.

For example, a person might start as a client service associate, then progress to a senior client service associate, a client service associate manager, an assistant manager, a director, and ultimately a regional vice president. Each progression is built on the organization's and department's growth, enabling us to meet our objectives effectively.

In my experience, the optimal span of control is around four to seven direct reports. Currently, I manage three reports and find that this allows me to conduct three effective meetings that drive our business forward. When each manager has around seven reports, it enables them to hold meaningful one-on-one meetings and provide valuable feedback, which aids in the development of team members as part of their daily operations. However, when managers are stretched too thin, they risk becoming overwhelmed and ineffective.

Many of us have encountered managers who appear busy: they come in early and leave late, yet still struggle to complete their tasks. This inefficiency often stems from being "deep as a puddle." They spread themselves too thin and are unable to focus effectively on their responsibilities.

The reason for this is that we haven't granted the autonomy necessary for Level Four leadership to effectively understand and manage the span of control. The ultimate goal is to develop leaders who can cultivate other leaders. That is how you know that you've established a strong leadership culture.

When everyone in management sees their role as identifying and mentoring someone who can eventually succeed them, the organization flourishes. Unfortunately, many cultures struggle with this because people often fear that developing others will jeopardize their own job security. We need to shift this mindset and help people understand that nurturing talent does not threaten their position. Instead, it should empower them to rise above their current roles and help the organization grow and thrive at an accelerated pace.

I want to address two key points. First and foremost, everyone in the organization reports up the hierarchy. Regardless of your position, you have a boss and a responsibility to prepare.

In our organization, whether you're a brand-new financial advisor or in any other entry-level role, you report to the district manager. The chain of reporting continues: the district manager reports to the assistant vice president (AVP), who reports to the first vice president (FVP), then to the regional vice president (RVP), followed by the senior vice president (SVP), and finally to me.

Each person must complete a report detailing their goals, KPIs, and whether they achieved them. For those who are early in their careers, meaning they have less tenure, the frequency of preparation and review should be more concentrated.

When someone is new, we often say that a day in their life is equivalent to a week, a week is like a month, a month is like a quarter, and a quarter is like a year. Over time, the volatility of their performance and their need for support will decrease. At a minimum, new employees should have two one-on-one meetings per week; this is critical. As they settle in, this can change to at least one meeting per week.

We have established a structured meeting framework because I've heard it said that no organization fails due to having too many meetings; rather, they often fail because they don't have enough.

In addition to the one-on-one meetings, we also implement monthly and quarterly structures. We call these strategic team meetings, which consolidate one-on-one updates and present them to a group. Furthermore, we conduct periodic business reviews, wherein monthly meetings are summarized into quarterly meetings to set targets for the upcoming quarter, which align with our one-on-one sessions.

To summarize: when a new employee joins, they should have two one-on-one meetings per week. After a few months, this can drop to one meeting per week. Additionally, everyone needs to maintain a monthly and quarterly schedule for their objectives.

This is a challenging situation. You start to realize there's an issue when there's a line of people outside your door with questions for you every minute of every day, and they seem unable to make decisions on their own. If you find yourself constantly bombarded by people who depend on you to perform tasks, that indicates a problem.

The issue isn't with the people; it's a systems problem. Specifically, it means you have not created a structure that encourages personal development. You need to ask yourself: *What am I doing to personally grow? What steps am I taking to achieve my goals? How am I aligning my efforts with the company's goals? What regular activities am I engaging in to develop as an individual?*

When I was responsible for multiple roles, including accountant, sales representative, and marketing team member, I frequently encountered requests from others asking, "How do I do this?" or "How do I do that?"

To resolve this, the first thing I did was seek coaching. Finding an executive coach who had successfully scaled a business was crucial. I began studying the practices of businesses that had effectively scaled. It became glaringly obvious that I was working sixty hours a week while my staff and employees were working forty hours a week. Something needed to change. It's essential to take a hard look at this situation and figure out how to make improvements.

You don't have time not to train. Covey refers to this as Quadrant II, which encompasses activities that are important but not urgent. If you frequently find yourself in Covey's Quadrant I, dealing with urgent and important tasks, like the fires of the day or the questions of the minute, you might want to ask yourself why people keep coming back to you with the same issues.

The reason is that you don't have a proper playbook. It would be much more beneficial to use Level Four leadership skills, which enable you to mobilize a group of people to solve problems consistently without requiring your constant involvement. This approach should be aligned with the mission, vision, and values of the organization.

To achieve this, bring your team together in a room, state the problem clearly, and ask them how you and they can solve it permanently. This way, they can contribute to the solution rather than relying on you to dictate it.

I refer to this phenomenon as "labeling," which refers to our inherent biases or prejudices towards others. Once we label someone, that label often becomes a self-fulfilling prophecy, as it leads to quick judgments about how we perceive that person. Throughout my life, I have discovered that whenever I labeled someone or formed an opinion about them, getting to know them personally changed my perspective. By understanding their values, goals, aspirations, and backstories, I often realized that my initial impressions were incorrect.

The first piece of advice I would give to you is this: whenever you think negatively about someone, whether you consider them lazy, unintelligent, inattentive, or lacking potential, you should reframe the way you approach the situation. Ask yourself a different question: *If this person were my brother, mother, or best friend and my role was to help them succeed, what would I be willing to do? Would I go out of my way to support their success?*

People can sense the genuine care and affection behind your intentions. Instead of labeling someone a failure for being late, address the concern more constructively. You might say, "I see so much talent in you, and I believe you have great potential. However, I've noticed that you struggle to arrive on time. Is there something I can do to help you with this?"

If, after sharing that concern, the person still arrives late the next day, you could say, "I realize that getting up in the morning is a challenge for you. I don't want this to hinder your career progress. Would it be all right if I helped you find a solution?" You could then suggest, "How about I give you a call in the morning to help ensure you get up on time? I really want to see you succeed."

Say the next day goes by, and when you call, they don't answer and show up late. By the third time, you might say, "This is disappointing. It's my mistake, too. I know I called, and you know it, too, but maybe your phone wasn't on, or something else happened. So, can I make a suggestion? I can't have you showing up late, and as your leader, I want to help prevent this from becoming a problem for you in your career. How about this? Your apartment is on my way home. Would you mind if I came to pick you up in the morning? Would that work for you?"

What I've found is that if a leader is willing to go the extra mile to support their employee in a positive way, that employee tends to become loyal to them. They think, *I know I'll be on time because my boss is looking out for me.*

It starts with the decision to be supportive in helping someone change their behavior. If you believe in people without labeling them, gossiping about them, or giving up hope, you will soon find that they will rise to the occasion.

Chapter 5

DELEGATE OR DIE

One of the challenges every business owner faces is that they can become their own biggest obstacle, a phenomenon I refer to as the "law of the lid." We've all heard that we are perfectly aligned with the results we achieve. When you are the founder of an organization and start experiencing success, the instinct is to hold on to that success as tightly as possible. However, the real challenge is learning to let go of control of the organization, not of clarity.

Control can feel safe, but it often becomes your greatest challenge. If you find yourself being a control freak, you limit other people's ability to achieve success and make their own decisions. This means you are left to make decisions for them, which creates a cycle of dependence. I often say, "Control equals comfort, which equals stagnation."

Trying to control every aspect of your business leads to comfort and stagnation. By doing so, you're essentially building walls that prevent you from growing and scaling your business.

For example, eight years ago, my team took a chance on ourselves. Fast forward to today, and we have grown to six hundred advisors across thirty-four offices in eighteen states.

Many people entering this field start with just one or two clients and a small staff, and they actively meet with clients. I haven't met with a client in five years.

What made the difference? It was my vision of relinquishing control and empowering others to achieve their goals. This mindset accelerated my growth. It's important to recognize that excessive control can limit everyone's ability to move forward.

Discomfort is often a precursor to growth and scaling. I frequently ask people whether they would rather be comfortable or uncomfortable. When faced with these two options, most people respond that they want to be comfortable. But if I rephrase the question to ask if they would prefer to grow or remain comfortable, many recognize that they would choose growth.

The natural consequence of growth and scaling is discomfort. If you can give people the autonomy they need to grow, they will thrive. However, if you stifle their growth by dismissing their ideas or sticking rigidly to "the way we do things around here," you inhibit their potential and, consequently, your own.

You're going to get yourself in trouble if you don't pay attention. There's a widely known experiment called "Five Apes in the Cage." The story goes like this: researchers have a cage with a stool in the middle and a banana hanging at the top.

First, they put one ape in the cage. When the ape tries to climb the stool to get the banana, it gets hosed down with water. Next, they introduce a second ape. As the second ape goes for the banana, it gets hosed down, too. Then they add a third ape, and when it attempts to get the banana, the same thing happens: it gets hosed down.

By this point, the first two apes are irritated by the experience. When researchers put a fourth ape in the cage, it tried to go for the banana, too, but the first two apes beat it up to stop it from climbing the stool. The third ape is confused and doesn't understand what's happening.

Next, the researchers add a fifth ape. As it goes for the banana, all the other apes team up to beat it up, even though the fifth ape has never experienced the hosing down. They continue this experiment, replacing one ape at a time, until eventually, whenever a new ape comes into the cage, all the other apes beat it up without knowing why. It becomes a case of "monkey see, monkey do."

This raises a question: why do we engage in behaviors like this? One example I can relate to is the story of how a family cooked ham by cutting it on both sides before putting it in the pan. One day, someone asked why they did that, and the answer was, "That's what our mom used to do."

When they called their mom, she explained that the only reason she cut the ham like that was that she didn't have a pan big enough to hold it. However, that original reason had been forgotten over time. This demonstrates how tradition without reason can stifle innovation.

We must constantly challenge assumptions and delegate goals while giving people the autonomy to find solutions. Overcontrolling leaders can stifle their organizations without realizing it. They may hesitate to hire or promote people because they believe they aren't ready. When a leader thinks, *Nobody can do it quite as well as I can*, they become the problem within the organization.

Unless you start thinking differently about how to delegate goals and let others find their own solutions, you will remain a constraint on your business. Teach people how to think, not just what to do; focus on the psychology of doing versus delegating.

Here's the ego trap: High performers often resist delegation because their identity is tied to completing tasks. They tend to hold on to their responsibilities, believing that their contributions define their success. However, the truth is that fostering leadership and embracing delegation leads to even greater performance. The more you delegate and trust others to take on those responsibilities, the more time you have.

You should think not only about assigning tasks but also about empowering others to own their work while being available to support them. If they fail to execute a task and rely on you to take it over, then the question arises: What do you need them for? It's essential that people understand their roles and responsibilities.

I often found myself in an ongoing battle with one of the principals in a company we acquired. My goal was to understand his vision, values, and leadership level so that we could grow the business. This founder had been with the organization for thirteen years. When we asked what systems were functioning well and which ones were not, you would have thought I had insulted him deeply.

He resisted any change, fearing it would undermine his legacy. A scarcity mindset hindered our ability to scale. In his mind, every initiative we proposed would threaten the business. But the issue wasn't about what we wanted to implement; it was the mindset of someone who believed that the only viable way to operate was the way he had done it for years.

Most people don't realize that the more they delegate, the more time they create for themselves to accomplish critical tasks. This misconception is purely a mindset issue. If you're bogged down with tasks every day, you won't have time to focus on planning the business's future or developing your strategy.

Additionally, it's important to delegate tasks that require low skill so you can focus on higher-level responsibilities.

This serves as a guideline for evaluating tasks. Whenever I question whether I should handle a specific task, I consider its skill level and time requirements; if it's low-skilled and time-consuming, delegating it is usually the best choice.

Tasks that can be performed by someone else with little training should be assigned to them. Additionally, any process-oriented tasks that require significant time and attention to detail, such as projects, reporting, or forecasting, are ideal for delegation. These types of projects allow people to demonstrate their abilities.

For example, I don't manage my own bookkeeping. While I have the capability to do so, I prefer not to. If I'm focused on bookkeeping, I'm not training leaders, reviewing our projects, or negotiating new contracts. So, even though I can execute these tasks well, I choose not to.

Here's my filter for evaluating tasks:

1. I ask myself, *Can I do it?* It doesn't matter if the answer is yes or no; I simply need to ask myself if I can.

2. If I can't do it, I find someone who can.

3. If I can do it, I then ask, *Can I train someone else to do it? Is this a task that, with a little guidance, could be handled by someone else?*

4. Another important question is: *Should someone else already be doing it?* If the answer to any of these questions is yes, it's time to delegate the task.

When I examine the organizational structure, I consider the org chart and the roles of team members. I ask myself whether there are tasks I am currently handling that others would be willing to take on, as this would provide them with more responsibility and opportunities for growth. If the answer is yes, I need to delegate those tasks accordingly.

Here are the types of tasks I typically delegate:

- Anything that is low-skill and repetitive.
- Process-oriented tasks that others can complete at 80 percent of my quality level. It's essential to avoid perfectionism. If a task isn't performed to my standards but still fulfills its purpose, such as meeting client needs or achieving an objective, it should be delegated.

To facilitate this process, I recommend using something called the "impact filter." If you search for "impact filter" online, you will find a valuable tool that everyone can use and rally around.

The concept was developed by Dan Sullivan, and it begins by answering a fundamental question: What is the project? This question is crucial, especially when hiring someone or creating a new role.

I've observed that many people simply copy a job description, post it online, and hire candidates based on their initial impressions. However, it's essential to consider more than just the title and description. We need to think about what a typical day in the role will look like, what success will entail, and what the consequences might be if we do nothing or take action.

The impact filter encourages us to define the project clearly, whether it's hiring a new team member, implementing a new process, or anything else pertinent to the business. We should start by envisioning what success would look like in six months to a year, establishing specific, measurable, actionable, realistic, and time-bound goals to define what success truly means.

Additionally, we need to consider the implications of inaction. What are the potential consequences of failing to hire the right people, establish effective processes, or create necessary documentation? Not addressing these issues might lead to problems like time creep, burnout, stagnation, or an inability to grow due to our fears about expansion.

Conversely, what positive outcomes can we expect if we proceed? How will taking action enable us to accomplish our goals? What will it free up for us, and how will it facilitate our progress?

A key element in this process is identifying the specific steps required to complete the project. This aspect can be challenging, as it requires careful thought and planning. When delegating tasks, ensure the person understands the specific action items and deadlines required to achieve success.

The takeaway here is that delegation serves as a multiplier. It allows you to move away from merely performing tasks and shifts your focus toward strategic growth for your business. By developing leaders and fostering your own growth, you can create Level Four and Level Five leaders within your organization. This transformation makes running your business more manageable and positions you as the maestro, orchestrating the efforts of your team rather than being the one playing every instrument.

I believe this is a matter of scarcity mentality. When you teach people how to think rather than just instruct them on what to do, it affects their self-worth. For example, when I do something, it makes me feel valuable, and giving that task away can make me feel as if I am no longer valued.

I have team members who may perceive even the smallest change, like the removal of a task, as a threat to their job security. They might feel upset or depressed, believing they are getting fired, when in reality, I am trying to create space for them to take on more meaningful work. I want them to focus on more valuable tasks, but to them, the original task is tied to their identity.

They believe that the tasks they handle define their worth and contribution to the company, when in truth, that's not the case.

Ultimately, the vision and business you've created can become a kind of prison for you. This is why many businesses grow rapidly, up to 50 percent a year, initially, but as they expand, they often find it challenging to maintain even a 10 percent growth rate.

When I first started the business, I noticed a common pattern among many founders: they tend to apply what they've learned in their own careers to their new ventures. This is how they grew and achieved success in the first place. For example, in the system I was familiar with, we had a structured hierarchy for developing leaders. You would start by training a district manager, then promote them to field vice president, then to group vice president, and finally to senior vice president. This was simply the way things were done.

During one meeting, we found ourselves trying to categorize everyone by how many people they managed, their production levels, and the responsibilities associated with each position. As a self-determining corporation, we began to question why we were limiting our roles and responsibilities. If our existing structure was making it difficult to meet our objectives, we needed to consider creating new roles and opportunities.

One of the lower-level managers shared an idea from their experience at Enterprise Rent-a-Car. They had a management trainee program with seven different levels, enabling employees to grow and advance more quickly. This was a pivotal moment for us. We realized we were constrained by traditional titles and responsibilities, which hindered our ability to scale leadership within the business.

All it took was an open-minded perspective from someone willing to share how another successful company operated. We took those insights and applied them to help us move beyond our limitations in developing leaders and redefining the roles associated with leadership.

Let's rewind to six years ago. This moment was a major turning point for our business. It enabled us to expand and grow in ways we hadn't anticipated, as different people took on various roles and traveled across the country. This flexibility significantly accelerated our growth.

If we had been resistant to change, insisting on "this is how we do things around here," we would have missed this opportunity. Being open to change allowed us to adapt and implement strategies that facilitated our business expansion.

How has delegating brought me freedom? Well, today, I do not engage in any task work. It took me a long time to feel comfortable letting go of tasks I used to rely on to fill my day, which I later realized weren't actually driving the important aspects of my business.

Now my role focuses on strategic leadership rather than day-to-day operations. Thanks to everything we've discussed, such as span of control, effective one-on-ones, structured leadership, and feedback loops, I strive to embody Level Five leadership while also developing Level Four leadership in others. I have very few scheduled tasks or meetings in my calendar, which is a testament to my ability to delegate what I once handled myself.

This delegation has enabled me to become a strategic business leader who "inspects what I expect," which has brought me to the next stage of my journey. It has freed me up to enjoy life on my terms; I can create my own schedule, take trips whenever I choose, and work from home. I even have time to play golf because I no longer have the direct tasks that once consumed my time.

Chapter 6

STAYING CLOSE TO THE WORK

The next area I want to discuss is staying close to the work. This is especially important for anyone in a leadership role or who is an organization founder. When you start to experience success, it's easy to become distant from the day-to-day operations.

Let's assume for a moment that you have a successful business with great people working around you. You have time and resources at your disposal, which can lead to the temptation to empower others to manage processes and make decisions. However, one of the challenges you might face is that even with the best processes in place, people still need to implement them effectively.

It's a natural human tendency, even when trained and knowing the correct procedures, to seek change, especially after performing tasks repeatedly. This is where leaders often find themselves at risk. As they become more successful or as the business grows, they tend to drift further away from the work itself. This distance can lead to declining performance, as it becomes challenging to identify and address problems effectively.

The show *Undercover Boss* illustrates this point well. In it, the boss of a company, facing issues within the business, goes undercover as an employee to gain firsthand experience. By working in various departments, they discover the realities that they were previously unaware of, revealing opportunities for improvement.

Ultimately, a leader loses their authority to lead when they do not understand how the work is done. This understanding is crucial for effective leadership.

A good friend and peer once said to me, "Jason, if you can't run the computer program that everybody needs, then you've lost your relevance."

We've all encountered bosses who say, "Do as I say," without having done that work themselves in years or being able to do it if needed. They might tell you to follow their instructions because they can no longer perform those tasks themselves. It's crucial to stay close to the work; otherwise, you risk losing your right to lead.

If you're in sales and can't make a sales call or don't know how to present or sell a product or service, you lose the credibility necessary to lead others. As a founder, you may not worry about this as much, but for other leaders in the organization, someone who can actually do the work will gain more credibility and may ultimately take their job.

One key principle is to "inspect what you expect." I learned this from the aforementioned Teresa Hanratty, who used to say that when results aren't meeting expectations, you need to look closely at the outcomes. When people claim they're doing everything asked but the results are lacking, the two most powerful words in leadership are "Show me."

To inspect what you expect means identifying where the problem lies in the person's work. This process can be thought of like the game Jenga: you pull out blocks one at a time, but the removal of just one block can cause the entire tower to fall. Your goal is to find that critical block by examining every step in the process. When you do this, you ask the person closest to the work to show you what they're doing so you can pinpoint the issue.

A top executive taught me that if you don't know what your team does every day, you lose your right to lead them. As an organization grows, leaders often drift away from the front lines. When there's strong leadership in place, team members insulate you from problems. I've encountered situations where leaders approached me with significant issues, and when I asked them, "Why didn't you bring this to me earlier?"

They replied, "We didn't want to bother you with our problems; you've hired us to fix them."

It's important to foster a culture where team members feel comfortable sharing their challenges rather than thinking you are too far removed to help.

To cultivate a culture where team members bring issues to you because they recognize your awareness and oversight, it's essential to remain engaged with the core tasks of your business. I encourage you to resist any tendency to drift away from these responsibilities with all your strength.

The "Pareto Principle," often misstated as the "Parade Principle," teaches us that 80 percent of results come from the most effective 20 percent of the people. In many executive leadership roles, there comes a time when a leader may feel out of place due to a lack of competence.

We have all worked under someone who was once effective but, over time, has left us wondering how they still hold their position. I witness this regularly as someone partially acquired by a private equity firm. Some individuals occupy roles without knowing how to solve problems or connect with the work being done.

These people often seek external reasons for underperformance, failing to recognize that their distance from the work is the issue. They have been promoted to their level of incompetence. Often, people without performance will begin to blame others rather than understanding that they are the only ones who can fix the issues. They use politics, markets, and macroeconomics as excuses, but these factors are rarely the cause. The problem is the leader's ability to look in the mirror and execute, especially if they are not intimately familiar with the work being completed.

Staying engaged allows for empathy. It shows your team that you genuinely care about the work. It also ensures accuracy, as you'll be able to quickly identify any drift from targets, keeping data on track.

Moreover, being close to the work fosters innovation. When you interact closely with those who perform the tasks daily, you open channels for listening to their ideas, which can lead to process improvements. It also helps you prevent changes that might worsen situations without your awareness.

More often than not, innovation springs from those closest to the work. When you ask, "Is there anything we can improve?" they typically have valuable insights. You can evaluate the merit of these ideas and develop them from a management perspective, particularly when you understand the ground-level operations.

By staying informed about your business operations, you can quickly identify when something is amiss. I've noticed revenue slippage reflected in profit-and-loss statements, especially when multiple factors were involved. We conduct forecasts every month, analyzing data month over month and year over year, which allows us to pinpoint problems efficiently.

I've encountered situations where, when I dug into the details, I discovered an accounting misclassification. It's easy to fix, but identifying such issues only happens if I stay engaged with the specifics. If you're a sales leader and you're not present on the floor, you might find that during meetings, your team members will rationalize their work. Even if their explanations don't make sense, it's essential for them to articulate their problems in a way that resonates with you as their leader.

This kind of understanding is impossible if you remain distanced from the work. I often tell young leaders that as organizations grow and their span of control increases, it's crucial to maintain a clear calendar to allow time for what we call "management by walking around" (MBWA).

Being on the floor gives you firsthand insight; it ensures you're not just hearing from subordinates but also observing the reality of the situation. One of the important aspects of staying close to the work is its impact on culture, both positively and negatively. Distance can lead to cultural drift.

If you're absent from the organization and not continually engaged in meetings that discuss vision, values, and mission, you may lose touch with your team's progress on objectives. This disconnect could undermine the management structure and allow your culture to drift away from the norms we previously established. If you're not personally involved, cultural changes will inevitably occur without your influence, and it becomes your responsibility to be the "culture king."

As a leadership example, I host weekly Zoom classes for our team. Everyone in the firm is required to attend these sessions, which focus on personal development. This platform allows my team to see me, and I can communicate directly with them. I emphasize that they can reach out to me anytime, whether through call, email, or text; my door is always open. If someone wants to schedule a meeting, they can simply email my staff to arrange it.

Another important thing during this communication, other than mission and vision, is the values of the organization.

Values are the fabric that allows the operation to know at a fundamental level what things are non-negotiable. While norms can change, values are the stitching of the fabric that keeps everybody working toward the mission and vision of the company.

I strive to convey the message that my role as CEO doesn't mean I'm out of touch with what's happening. This approach fosters comfort within the team, showing them that I have their backs. It also breaks down hierarchical barriers; if someone has an issue, they know they can come to me.

Recently, a senior vice president reached out because he was feeling significant pressure from a regional vice president. Instead of trying to circumvent the senior vice president, he called me for guidance on how to handle the situation effectively. This open line of communication demonstrates the strength of our relationship and allows for collaborative problem-solving.

That's the type of feedback I need to know. I'm gathering all sides of the story to effectively course correct. Integrity and servitude are the highest values of leadership.

"The servant's towel can never be too big." You need to respect those who are willing to take bullets, punches, and arrows for the team. This is how you earn your team's respect.

So, what is integrity? I define it in a couple of ways. First, do what you say you're going to do. Second, don't lie to yourself. This is the worst level of integrity, when you promise something but fail to follow through, or when your behavior doesn't align with your words.

Servitude is about understanding our organizational structure. If I showed you our org chart, you would see that the CEO is at the bottom, the senior vice presidents are at the bottom, and the client is at the top. Everyone else supports that structure.

As a leader of an organization that was acquired by a private equity firm, I continue to remind the firm's CEO: who is the client? I don't serve them; they serve me. My people do not serve me as the CEO; I serve them. My job is to help them reach the highest possible level in their careers and lives.

I respect that my team members take bullets, punches, and arrows because I'm willing to do the same alongside them. I want to be involved and engaged in all aspects of the business, whether it's a sales call or meetings with finance or compliance. I'm ready to face challenges, including meetings with regulators.

Quick story about sales conversion: our sales conversion rate went from five to one, meaning when we met five new prospects, one of them became a client. However, we started drifting to a seven-to-one conversion rate. While that may seem like a small change, moving from five to seven represents a 30 percent dip in conversion, translating to a 30 percent reduction in clients and revenue.

Whenever I see this happening, I step in and hijack a team member's training session. We have daily classes and training, and I step in to ask questions and identify basic areas for improvement. By retraining them, we can recover our conversion rates.

For instance, we found that people weren't sending calendar invites via email, weren't texting reminders, and many were not using their cameras during Zoom meetings, leaving us talking to a black screen. We must not neglect the basics.

To ensure that you stay connected to the fundamentals of your business, remain closely involved in the daily operations. As a founder, you should actively engage with your team. In today's work-from-home environment, this can mean participating in virtual meetings.

For instance, consider implementing a company-wide Zoom calendar and make an effort to join these calls to see what's happening. Staying engaged will help you maintain your skills and stay sharp. It's crucial to remain proficient in the core tasks that contributed to your initial success.

When we started our business, I had to excel in recruiting, delivering presentations, and making sales. I'm proud to say that eight years later, I still excel in recruiting, sales, and the fundamental tasks that have made the business thrive. The further you stray from the front lines, the more your decision-making can suffer.

If you don't stay close to the work, you lose the insights needed to make informed decisions.

Each department has KPIs that help measure success. There are three components that define these KPIs: activity, conversion, and results. Activity refers to the amount of work being done, conversion measures how that activity leads to outcomes, and results reflect the overall success. We often express this relationship as follows:

Activity × Conversion × Case Size = Result

To effectively measure performance, focus on these three components. In our business, we identify six key activities that are crucial for driving results:

1. Generating a Lead: Identifying potential customers who need to learn about our offerings.
2. Calling the Prospect: Reaching out to these leads to engage them.
3. Meeting the Prospect: Interacting with the potential customer face-to-face.
4. Case Analysis or Proposal Preparation: Preparing a proposal tailored to their needs.

5. Presenting the Proposal: Presenting the solution and detailing the product or service to the prospect.

6. Servicing the Client: Ensuring that the client is satisfied and continues to do business with us.

Regardless of the industry, whether you're at Mercedes-Benz or Cracker Barrel, these steps remain consistent. You must generate leads, reach out to them, meet with them, build and present a compelling proposal, and provide excellent service to retain their business.

By focusing intently on these key activities, you can effectively drive the success of your business. Remember, it's the combination of activity, conversion, and average revenue per transaction that ultimately determines your overall success.

Once you understand the key activities and their associated metrics, you need a system to measure where things are breaking down. For instance, is the issue occurring during phone calls or in face-to-face meetings? Establish target ratios for these interactions.

If you don't have those ratios, you can perform a bottleneck analysis. It's essential to teach everyone how to conduct this analysis. Essentially, bottleneck analysis involves asking, "Why aren't we achieving this result?" and determining where the breakdown is occurring in the system. By getting close to the work, you can identify the specific areas that need fixing.

It's also important to determine where people are in their development process. There are four different stages of development: D1, D2, D3, and D4. Alongside these stages, we categorize leadership styles as S1, S2, S3, and S4. In our leadership development training, we teach how to identify where people are in their development and what type of leadership they need at that stage.

The D1 stage is known as the "enthusiastic beginner." It's important to remember that this categorization is always task-specific.

Think about it: when you start a new job or learn a new task, you're taking on new responsibilities. For example, when a manager tells you, "Sarah, I want you to learn how to do this," you enter the situation bright-eyed and eager. You might feel hopeful, inexperienced, curious, and optimistic. You're excited about learning new tasks and show a strong eagerness and enthusiasm.

In this D1 stage, you have low competence because you've never done the task before, but you possess high commitment and a desire to learn. We all know people like this, right?

The leadership style suitable for D1 is a coaching method known as "show, tell, do." With this approach, you first show the person how to complete the task, then tell them what you did, and finally ask them to try it themselves.

Let's move on to the second stage, D2, known as the "disillusioned learner." People in this phase often feel overwhelmed, confused, demotivated, and frustrated. They may experience moments of competence but are not yet proficient. Because they lack both reliable skills and commitment, they might start to doubt whether the task is right for them and may even consider quitting.

In summary, D2 learners possess some skills but face challenges that lead to feelings of discouragement. They require reassurance as they navigate through this phase, unsure whether they still want to learn this task or whether their frustration stems from issues with their boss and manager. They tend to make excuses and lash out. What these people really need is love and attention.

You can't just delegate work to them or constantly micromanage them. It's essential to engage them and ask about the challenges they face. You need to coach them, finding a balance between micromanagement and guiding them on their current tasks.

The most important thing is to help them progress through their current stage as quickly as possible by enhancing their skills through effective leadership. For example, if you have two one-on-one meetings a week and they're still struggling, consider increasing it to three meetings. You want to provide direct feedback frequently while encouraging them to tackle tasks one step at a time.

In this context, we refer to D3 as a capable, cautious performer. These people are self-critical, cautious, and doubtful, yet they are capable. They can contribute, but they often feel insecure and tentative and may appear bored or apathetic. They possess moderate to high competence, meaning they can do the job, but their commitment varies, leaving them uncertain about whether they want to continue.

Many of these people are just frustrated because they lack confidence. What they need is support and encouragement. Rather than micromanaging, ask them, "What would you do?" When they provide an answer, affirm it by saying, "That's exactly what you should do; great job!"

I liken this to how parents respond when a child falls. One type of parent rushes over, causing the child to cry. The other responds with excitement, which encourages the child to laugh and get back up. As a leader, your role is not to micromanage or be overly forceful, but to coach and uplift that person by acknowledging their efforts.

Ultimately, we all aspire to reach the D4 stage, becoming self-reliant achievers who are justifiably confident, consistently competent, and capable of inspiring others. These people are highly competent and committed. You never want to micromanage someone at this level. Instead, encourage them to lead and mentor others.

The worst thing you can do is hold someone back. It's vital to let talented individuals soar. Everyone desires to be a self-reliant achiever, and teams benefit tremendously from having such members. Remember, the focus should be on task-specific growth rather than personality traits.

To effectively retain employees, we train our leaders to assess their team members using two key criteria: commitment and skill level. Specifically, we categorize people as having low or high commitment and low or high skill. Understanding which stage each employee is in provides a benchmark for leaders. This way, they can avoid micromanaging and instead apply the appropriate leadership style to ensure tasks are completed effectively, empowering employees rather than micromanaging them.

My dad was a pastor. From a young age, the principles of the Bible were instilled in me, particularly to treat others as I would like to be treated. Because of this upbringing, I'm the type of person who would give you the shirt off my back, even if it means going without.

We lived in a very poor community. My father started our church in our home. Eventually, it grew to occupy an auditorium, then an office building, and finally, he built a church from the ground up. Our home often served as a refuge; it wasn't uncommon for my dad to bring homeless people to the house, and some would stay on our couch for weeks at a time. Service and humility were central to our family life.

I learned the value of servant leadership. There's a saying that your servant's towel can't be too large. Over time, I've come to understand this value deeply: when you selflessly help others with a sincere heart, aiming to help them achieve their own goals, an unintended consequence is that you often get what you want in return. Giving is, in a way, a selfish act because it brings satisfaction and joy to the giver. It's a natural human behavior to feel good when we do good for others.

This principle of servitude connects back to the mission of my company, which is to help people reach the highest possible level in their careers and lives. I genuinely believe in this mission and often share stories that illustrate it.

What truly makes me happy and motivates me to get up every day for work is watching young women become successful, powerful, and confident. I also enjoy witnessing young men, including those from fraternal backgrounds, transform into remarkable, compassionate human beings. My mission, vision, and values center on serving these individuals. This doesn't mean I do everything for them; rather, I provide them with a platform, coaching, and the mindset training necessary to become good people.

In turn, this commitment helps me become a better person. To me, integrity is about being honest with yourself about who you are. Many people say one thing, but their actions and beliefs often contradict their words. For instance, someone might claim they want to be wildly successful while refusing to wake up early, leave work late, or put in effort on weekends. They may also shy away from constructive feedback or avoid reading to grow.

This lack of alignment is what I refer to when I speak of integrity. It's crucial not to deceive yourself about your character or your level of commitment to your goals. When you stop lying to yourself about who you are and what you are willing to do, you will unlock your full potential.

PHASE
Three

*(Real businesses don't rely on heroes.
They rely on rhythm.)*

Chapter 7

BUILD THE SCOREBOARD

Phase three of the platform typically spans years five through eight. In this stage, we focus on systems and superstars. First, let's define what a "superstar" is and explain why having too many of them may not be beneficial.

Real businesses don't rely on heroes; they rely on rhythm. The goal is to establish a rhythm that allows your business to scale and accelerate growth. This involves maximizing people's performance without limiting them, so you can continue expanding your business.

In my conversations with many business leaders, a recurring theme is their struggle to hire the best possible candidates to delegate tasks and boost performance. However, there are only so many exceptional people available, and you must recognize that everyone else is also trying to recruit those same top talents. If a candidate is truly remarkable, they may be beyond your budget.

To illustrate this point, consider the example of growing up in New England and managing a business. Imagine if I could have a team full of Tom Bradys. The challenge in every sport and business is that there is only one Tom Brady, who is widely regarded as the greatest of all time. Even the best players, like Brady, may leave to join other teams due to factors like money, egos, and personalities.

Building a business solely around a group of rock stars is not a sustainable strategy. Instead, you need to develop a system that succeeds despite the absence of a superstar.

Bill Belichick once discussed this in relation to free agency. He emphasized that while Tom Brady played a crucial role in winning championships, a football team comprises a fifty-three-man roster. Each player is just as important, if not more so, than any single superstar. It's essential for the team to work cohesively and coordinate effectively to achieve continuous championship victories year after year.

Bill Belichick used to say that in the world of free agency, he had to rebuild his team every eighteen months. This is something I took to heart. I realized I couldn't rely on having the best players consistently perform; instead, I needed to develop a system to develop and enhance the best talent. The question then is, how do you build a system that outlasts individual players and continues to win, regardless of who is on the team?

The reality is, if you rely on ten outstanding players, you face a problem when they eventually leave. It's not just a "rockstar problem"; it's a recurring challenge that requires you to constantly rehire top talent. Rather than focusing solely on having superstars, I prefer to create a system that attracts ambitious people. I want people to clearly understand what is expected of them to move forward and to be obsessed with climbing the career ladder.

I want them to be competitive, hungry, and even a bit delusional at times. I encourage them to express their desire for advancement, saying things like, "I want your job." This mindset, cultivated within a strong organizational culture, can transform individuals into dedicated team members who are willing to go to great lengths to succeed.

To achieve this, you need robust systems in place. High-performing people thrive in structured environments, but if those systems are absent, they may resort to office politics and infighting, focusing on personalities rather than solving problems or achieving results. Therefore, it's essential to establish strong systems; otherwise, the organization may collapse.

Now, let's discuss some of the key systems. One important principle I always adhere to is that "what gets measured gets momentum." To ensure everyone knows their performance status at all times, you need to create a scorecard. The scorecard serves as an engine that allows people to track whether they are doing a good job.

The scorecard acts as a referee, indicating that regardless of how well you believe you're performing, the metrics used to measure KPIs may tell a different story. One of my former bosses, Sam Sansel, once said, "I appreciate your hard work, but what I respect is your results. I don't value hard work without results."

While I recognize the effort you put in, the focus must ultimately be on the results. The scorecard serves as an unbiased measuring stick; it doesn't take politics, personalities, or other factors into account.

I've spoken to many people about how to motivate others to complete specific tasks. They often think it's complicated, but it's really quite simple. As long as you measure activity, conversion rates, and the desired results, and you keep the process straightforward and transparent, meaning there's a regular reporting system tied to your objectives, everyone will know where they stand at all times.

When people understand where they stand, you'll find that the top performers in your organization will engage with the scorecard and treat it like a game. Transparency is crucial, especially for adults seeking to advance their careers. People dislike surprises, particularly when it comes to promotions; no one wants to feel disappointed after expecting a reward and not receiving one.

Consider a tennis player: repetitive practice leads to championships. Systems allow you to teach, scale, and track success consistently over long periods. Just like perfecting the same forehand and backhand, practice leads to improvement. Systems enable you to retrain through repetition, ensuring that your focus is appropriately directed.

This approach also allows people to progress steadily rather than experience erratic fluctuations in performance. In my organization, we have scorecards for everything. Everyone tracks their net annualized compensation (NAC), which is essential for paying bills and determining profit margin. We also monitor net gain, client retention, and clients per person; all of this is clearly defined and documented. Each week, we email these updates so everyone knows their standing.

If you don't establish your own scorecard, others will create theirs, which may not align with your objectives. It's essential to define your promotion model clearly.

Let's move on to promotions. This process helps to remove ego from the equation. When you have a system that measures everyone, people can clearly see where they stand in various aspects of their performance. This makes it easier to determine who is ready for promotion and who should be considered next.

Additionally, this system helps identify employees who may not be a good fit for the organization. Jack Welch, the former CEO of GE, famously implemented a scorecard system where he would fire the bottom 10 percent of performers each year and promote the top 10 percent. He noted that while this approach raises the performance bar over time, there will always be people at the bottom.

Ultimately, you need a scoreboard that provides transparency and fosters friendly competition. It's essential to teach people how to provide constructive feedback without creating resentment, as personal dynamics can affect the workplace environment.

An important aspect is coaching effectively without being harsh. Anyone can track numbers: Did you meet your targets? If not, why? However, true leadership involves helping individuals grow, even if they don't initially meet their objectives. A good friend once told me, "Feedback without relationship is harassment." This insight highlights the importance of empathy in creating a team-oriented environment. It's not about simply enforcing numbers; it's about encouraging personal development.

When you provide daily support and guidance, helping people improve their performance, they can master the scorecard and, in turn, teach others to do the same. This is where the true magic happens.

If your system is clear and effective, you can recruit anyone into a leadership role. We believe in prioritizing eagerness over readiness, which allows people to grow without undermining their peers.

It's crucial to train people on how to recruit others into leadership roles. In our organization, I make it a point to show potential recruits the company culture, how much money employees can earn, and exactly what they need to achieve to succeed.

We highlight the key competencies required for promotion and outline the steps needed to develop them. It's important to understand the daily actions necessary to reach those goals.

We define what success looks like on a weekly, monthly, quarterly, and yearly basis. Our focus is on establishing systems that help people attain these objectives. When expectations are clear, people are motivated to pursue their goals because they know exactly where they stand at all times.

To illustrate, consider Bill Belichick's analogy: in football, you have the opportunity to refresh your team every eighteen months. Implementing solid systems reduces reliance on individual talents. If the departure of a single person could jeopardize your company, it indicates a flaw in your systems.

Think about it like this: if someone being recruited away results in the loss of 20 percent of your revenue, then you are not operating a sustainable business capable of thriving in the long term.

Such an outcome reflects your limiting belief system as a leader.

What you want is eagerness over mere readiness. You will never truly be ready for the job you'll take on because you haven't experienced what it requires.

It's important to find someone who exhibits the right behaviors and norms that we discussed earlier. Then provide them with the coaching they need to succeed in that role. Additionally, we follow a strict policy of only hiring from within the organization.

We have never brought someone in from outside to take a position above existing employees who are striving for that same role. This approach is important because we have a clearly defined career path for everyone to follow. Promoting an external candidate over someone who has been working hard for that position goes against our values and frustrates our team. They wonder why someone from outside was chosen when they have been working diligently to earn that role themselves.

Our process starts with having a well-defined leadership path, so everyone understands what they need to achieve to progress, regardless of their tenure with the company or their current position. Our promotion system is not based on seniority or office politics. It is purely focused on meeting clear expectations.

There are two components to consider: results and behaviors. You can have someone who performs exceptionally well, but as Jack Welch would say, performance alone isn't enough. I once had a great performer whom I would frequently argue with. While he had strong results and was a good person, his behaviors and integrity posed challenges for me. I would often tell him, "You take up way too much space in my mind, regardless of your talent." If you have a talented person whose values don't align with your organization's, you need to consider letting them go.

There have been times when I've evaluated a scorecard with the top three people under consideration. The differences in their performances were marginal. In such cases, behaviors and values come into play. It becomes a matter of aligned values and results.

I had a boss named Larry Post, who was a mentor of mine in the financial services company where he held the title of group vice president. Above him was a senior vice president, and above that position was the CEO. I once had dinner with the CEO and Larry, who was responsible for recruiting and training about a dozen of the thirty-two group vice presidents and three out of four senior vice presidents. I asked the CEO why Larry wasn't the senior vice president or his successor.

Jim Cracciolo, the CEO, took a moment to think and then replied, "What we want is the results of Patton…"

I interjected, "But Jim, this is Patton! He's the most successful general in the history of Ameriprise and has created a factory of talent; he's a kingmaker!"

Jim then said, "What we're looking for is someone who has the results of Patton but the diplomacy of Eisenhower."

I've never forgotten that insight. It highlights that success isn't solely about results; it's also about how others perceive you and how you navigate relationships, which are part of the organizational norms. As a result, there have been instances where the number one candidate did not get the job, but the number three candidate did.

If that's the case, it will be clearly defined, and we use a subjective measure called an "L rating." Seventy-five percent of your scorecard is based on your results, which are very objective. Everyone knows what it is, and everything is measured.

The remaining 25 percent focuses on behavior and is rated on a scale from one to five. Essentially, this helps me define aspects of people's behavior that may frustrate me and that I want them to pay attention to. I provide a scorecard covering compliance, HR issues, professionalism, and related factors. This helps leaders understand why one person may receive higher recognition than another.

Another significant metric we consider for the L rating is the number of people you have promoted. It's not solely about your personal growth and results; it's also about how much you have contributed to the company by promoting others into different roles within the firm. This is a major factor in why one person may be considered for a higher position over another. They are seen as "kingmakers," helping others become better leaders while advancing their own careers.

It's not a given from the start; it evolves over time and is fundamentally designed to address the biggest business challenges you face today, in alignment with your growth and vision for the business. The best way to define these challenges and determine how to measure them is to involve the people closest to the work and eager to perform at high levels.

As I mentioned, our meeting structure consists of several components: a weekly one-on-one meeting, a weekly team meeting, a monthly strategic team meeting, a quarterly business review, a periodic business review (PBR), semi-annual planning sessions, and annual planning.

When you're trying to solve business challenges, the most effective approach is to bring your leadership team, regardless of title, together in a small group to discuss the challenges at hand. During these discussions, you can establish the metrics you want to follow, consider whether other metrics could be useful, and strategize on how to use these metrics to influence behavior and achieve results. Collaboration is key to developing the best possible scorecard.

Over time, as our organization has grown, there has been less input from others, but initially, it was crucial to gather feedback from various team members to evaluate the scorecard. Our scorecard includes several rankings that indicate acceptable and unacceptable levels of performance. It generates numerical results that help determine whether we are meeting our targets. For example, if the target for net sales increase is set at twenty to achieve what we call G1, which represents good results, and we only achieve ten, then our scorecard shows we are at only 50 percent of the potential performance.

The most important aspect is to involve everyone in this process. This aligns with the Level Four leadership concepts we discussed earlier in the book, which emphasize the ability to mobilize a group of people to consistently solve problems and achieve results. Mobilizing people means allowing them to have a say and to contribute to solving these issues.

Chapter 8

GROWING OTHER LEADERS

I always say that your ultimate goal should be to become the "king of kings." The true measure of your success, whether in terms of business growth or the platform you build, lies in how many people can run your business without your direct involvement.

First, you must realize that it's impossible to lead fifty people directly. A significant part of the challenge is recognizing whether you have become your own bottleneck. So, how do you identify that?

You'll notice that you are often the only person who can answer certain questions, with team members regularly coming to you for permission on almost everything. If you find that you have fifty people surrounding you every day, and there's a constant line of requests being funneled through your assistant for time on your calendar, this indicates that you have become the problem by not effectively growing new leaders.

When considering how to develop a team of fifty people, remember an important principle from business literature: the "span of control." This concept refers to the maximum number of direct reports a person can effectively manage, typically around seven. To build a strong leadership structure as your business grows, identify the new roles (at senior, director, or VP levels) needed, while always keeping the span of control in mind. In practice, effective management limits the number of people a person oversees to four.

To change this dynamic, you must first acknowledge that you have become a bottleneck in your organization. You need to stop trying to personally manage everyone. Realize that you can't carry the entire load yourself; instead, you must empower others to run and manage parts of the business.

The goal is to nurture captains and fellow leaders, not to gather a horde of followers. When I ask people to define leadership, many respond with "followership," implying it is about getting people to places they couldn't reach on their own. However, true leadership should be about cultivating captains, people who can not only steer the ship but also build it and train others to navigate it. These leaders should understand the mission and be ready to carry it out, even in your absence. Therefore, it is essential to equip and empower leaders within your organization.

To effectively lead, you need to guide leaders in becoming captains themselves. They should not just follow you; instead, they should emulate your leadership qualities. This can be achieved by empowering leaders to take ownership of their outcomes.

Many managers mistakenly believe that their role is simply to delegate tasks, assigning work like a human to-do list. This approach does not embody true leadership. In contrast, real leaders facilitate a leadership pipeline that eliminates management bottlenecks.

When you develop more people who are equipped to solve problems—leaders at Levels Two and Three—something significant happens: they won't need to constantly seek your approval for basic decisions, like when to take a break or how to perform their tasks. They start to realize that they are empowered to achieve their goals every day.

By cultivating other leaders, you create a workforce of problem solvers. This is accomplished through defining clear responsibilities, establishing a well-defined scorecard, and providing a leadership path that illustrates their potential. As you enter your office each day, remember to mentor your potential replacements regularly and early.

I often say that eagerness should take precedence over readiness. During a podcast with a successful young business owner, he asked me if there's ever a time when it's too early to promote someone into a leadership position. My answer is an emphatic "no."

In fact, I treat every new hire as if they are already in a leadership role. Everyone has the potential to lead, whether positively or negatively. It is my responsibility to guide them in demonstrating positive behaviors.

If someone impresses me by arriving early, staying late, excelling at their work, and meeting deadlines, I make a point of acknowledging their potential. I want to encourage that spark in them, letting them know that I see something special. Ultimately, my goal is to mentor them so they can eventually take on specific responsibilities within the business.

People appreciate being recognized for their talents and feel valued when their leaders encourage them to step into greater roles. So, remember, it is your responsibility to prioritize eagerness over readiness.

Find the good in what people are doing early and often. Encourage them to keep moving forward. Growth comes from multiplying leadership, not just adding more staff. Often, people think they need another staff member to resolve their issues. They may say, "I need another manager or someone to help with my to-do list," rather than considering how to develop more leaders who can make decisions aligned with their common objectives.

Adding another person to the team who is merely there to manage tasks doesn't lead to fulfillment; they may not find satisfaction in a role that doesn't allow them to pursue the best version of themselves. Therefore, it's crucial to develop your leadership bench.

Always be on the lookout for potential leaders. You become a greater asset when you teach others to perform their jobs, or even your own job, well, rather than trying to protect your position. Many leaders face challenges when they realize they haven't developed others; they can become overwhelmed, confused, and protective of their roles.

If you provide a clear definition of what growth looks like and how people can develop and potentially replace you, you'll foster an environment where leadership flourishes. When someone is promoted, it not only elevates that individual but also strengthens the organization as a whole. Building a robust leadership pipeline will propel your business to the next level.

I have many stories to share that illustrate this. One significant experience was when I started a scratch operation under the guidance of Teresa Hanratty, who later became a senior vice president at Ameriprise. She was a critical figure in my life, helping me grow as a leader.

When I was living in Portland, Maine, Teresa recognized my potential and encouraged me to move to Portsmouth, New Hampshire, to start a brand-new organization. I had little direction; my role was simply to recruit, train, and develop people to achieve specific business objectives.

I had always been good at working hard and recruiting others into a sales career. Within nine months, I successfully recruited twenty-four people, who all showed up on the same day, creating quite a situation. It was just me and twenty-four newcomers seeking guidance on various tasks and challenges.

The volume of inquiries was overwhelming. To manage this, I realized I needed additional support. I began identifying people who were showing the most progress and took them out to lunch. I told them, "I see you as the future of the organization. I will promote you, and eventually, you'll have my role, and then the one above that, and so on, until you reach the level of senior vice president. Are you on board with this?"

They enthusiastically agreed. I then outlined my expectations: I wanted them to stay later, work harder, study more, and train intensively to achieve specific results. Once they met those outcomes, I would promote them.

Another key principle I followed, which remains integral to our company today, is the philosophy of "do nothing alone." When training others, especially when everyone is approaching you with questions and issues, it's tempting to resolve one person's problem at a time. However, I encourage a collaborative approach to ensure everyone learns effectively.

If someone asks you, "Could you please show me how to do that?" have them first find three other people so you can all work on it together. By doing this, you create a culture of collaboration while training multiple people at the same time. You can guide them by saying, "I'm going to show you and these three other people how to do this." Then, when someone comes to you, ask them to show three other people the exact same thing.

When people do this effectively and achieve results, I will consider them for a promotion to another position. This is typically how the model works: identify potential early, assign them tasks that help them develop quickly, and simultaneously train them to train others whenever you're working on a specific task.

In this way, you won't have to handle things alone again.

I believe norms play a crucial role in defining behavior, as they are foundational to creating culture. However, many people lack explicit norms regarding expectations for behavior. For instance, if someone said something upsetting to me, I might feel frustrated and choose to establish a norm around it.

One of my key norms is "70 percent agree, 100 percent support." This means that we don't have to fully agree on everything we do. If you are at least 70 percent in agreement with a proposed plan, it may not be perfect for you, but it's acceptable. The question is, can you live with it? If the answer is yes, I expect you to provide 100 percent support for the strategy we implement in the workplace, as it helps us achieve our objectives.

If you feel you are less than 70 percent in agreement, let's say you're at 50 percent, I would ask you what you need to feel more comfortable. It's important to articulate what you support. For example, you might say, "I would support this plan if we added that." Then I would talk to other team members to gauge if they agree with the proposed addition and whether it brings them closer to the 70 percent threshold for consensus.

Another essential aspect of norms is that they provide a way to correct behavior. This established language means that when someone acts inappropriately, we can address it directly. For example, we have a standard that there are no excuses for being late to work or meetings; we call it "Lombardi time." Arriving on time means you are actually late, so we need to discuss how to support each other to arrive punctually.

Finally, we ask team members to regularly evaluate themselves regarding these norms. In our meetings, we distribute a self-assessment at least once a month, in which the person rates their adherence to the norms on a scale from one to ten. For instance, if you reflect on your punctuality over the past month and find you were late half the time, you'd rate yourself a five out of ten.

All of these norms are regularly assessed through self-evaluation. Then you ask, "What actions will you take over the next thirty days to improve one of the top-three norms related to your behavior? Additionally, what is your specific action plan to achieve these goals?"

This is how you maintain behavioral norms within your culture: through self-assessment of performance against those norms and a commitment to self-improvement. Each month, people should identify what they will do and the desired outcomes to consistently enhance their performance.

And then it keeps going. If they have problems with the norms, they are the problem, right?

The norms within a company serve as the foundation for expected behavior. Therefore, if you have an issue with these norms, it indicates a deeper problem. These standards help us define what constitutes appropriate behavior.

If someone strongly disagrees with these norms, they may need to leave the company. For instance, if you're someone who doesn't accept feedback, spends time scrolling on Instagram during work hours, consistently arrives late to meetings, or delivers subpar work despite efforts to address the issues, then you may not be a good cultural fit for the organization.

The goal is to avoid situations where an employee wakes up one day to find out it's their last day without having been given a chance to improve. When a leader comes to me wanting to fire someone for being late, I ask a crucial question: "What have you done as a leader to address this behavior?" I expect them to explain their efforts to help the employee change.

If no significant attempts have been made, I will suggest that we create a plan to help the employee improve. Ultimately, it starts with the leader's behavior and their understanding of their role in fostering the growth and development of their team members.

Teamwork makes the dream work.

There is no mistake in growing leaders too fast; the real mistake lies in growing leaders too slowly. This slow growth becomes the limiting factor for the business.

As a founder, you may create your own limitations by believing that no one can do things as well as you do. This frustration stems from the perception that others cannot replicate your success. Often, this issue arises because you are too slow to develop leaders and unclear about the expectations or benchmarks you have set. It can also be due to your inability to communicate what behaviors are preventing others from growing at the pace you desire. Ultimately, the responsibility for this stagnation lies with you as the founder.

A mentor of mine once told me, "What's interesting about life and leadership is that you eventually realize you are both the problem and the solution." If you find yourself frustrated with the results, ambition, or personal accountability of others, the first step is to look in the mirror and recognize that you have a role in this dynamic. You need to ask yourself what you are doing to improve the behaviors and outcomes of those around you.

Also, it's important to understand that readiness is subjective. Many people think, *I would hire someone else, but I can't find anyone qualified for the job.* This kind of thinking is a limiting mindset. You may believe someone isn't ready for a job simply because they haven't done it before, but their readiness can be established through other means. If a person understands the requirements of the job and shows up every day with a positive attitude, the willingness to learn, and a commitment to receive feedback, they can be successful in that role.

As a founder, your primary task is to identify people who exhibit positive behaviors and can adhere to established norms.

Once you find them, assign them responsibilities to gauge their performance, even if they initially feel unprepared. You might say, "I know you're not ready, but I'm going to give you a three-month trial period to achieve these objectives. I believe in your potential, and I'll be here to coach you and provide support whenever you need it."

It's crucial for founders to focus on finding the balance between recognizing a person's ability to perform a job, understanding the importance of their behavior, setting clear goals, and empowering them to pursue those objectives.

I was once interviewed on Chase Gruening's *CoachG* podcast. The interviewer, a former football coach and player, shared his vision of hiring top-tier athletes, like Tom Brady, to help build and scale his business. He lamented that he was struggling to find enough qualified people. I told him he was thinking about it all wrong.

As a Patriots fan, I used the example of when receiver Wes Welker went down, and Julian Edelman stepped up. I hadn't even heard of Edelman before, but he became a star on the field. Similarly, when tight end Ben Watson was injured, Rob Gronkowski took his place, and I didn't know who Gronkowski was either until he proved himself.

The key takeaway is that leaders develop talent rather than merely hire it. You don't just seek out skilled people; you bring in people who are aligned with the mission, vision, and values of your organization.

You should set clear expectations for how hard you want them to work and hire as many of these motivated people as you can, regardless of their backgrounds, experience, or academic performance. What matters most is their commitment to the vision and values of the organization. It's then your responsibility to provide them with the right tools, behaviors, and systems to grow into the people you need them to be.

In the insurance industry, there's a common saying: "Don't hire bad people." However, I often found myself in trouble during leadership sessions when I pushed back against this notion. First of all, nobody wants to be labeled a "green pea," and I don't think it's accurate to categorize people as simply good or bad. The real distinction lies in the quality of leadership.

If you can use interviews to determine who will be successful and who won't, you're likely much more perceptive than I am. My experience shows that the people I liked, though I was uncertain about their potential, have often outperformed expectations. Conversely, those I initially believed would excel have frequently underperformed. The key factor in these outcomes has consistently been the guidance they received from their leaders.

Good leaders tend to produce great results and cultivate strong teams, while bad leaders often lead to poor performance and disengaged employees. You could place a bad leader in a high-performing organization, and within a short time, that organization would begin to falter. On the other hand, if you place a good leader in a struggling organization, it will likely improve quickly. Ultimately, it all comes down to leadership effectiveness.

Chapter 9

SYSTEMIZE THE MAGIC

There comes a moment for every founder when they realize that they're not just creating a business; they've created a job for themselves. They've become the business, and that can be a painful realization.

They find themselves acting as the janitor, the marketing department, and the finance department. They're the ones answering everyone's questions, and every problem falls on their shoulders because no one else can solve them. This stems from the mindset that no one else can do it like they can. That needs a significant mentality shift.

I used to think the same way. I'm not here to judge anyone; it turns out that when you hold on to that belief, you unintentionally create limitations and end up sabotaging your growth.

In the early days, I believed the quickest way to scale was to control every decision. Whether it was managing the photocopier, handling IT issues, or making sure there was coffee in the refrigerator, my stubbornness took over. I became the recruiter, the trainer, the strategist, the IT specialist, the finance manager, and the compliance officer. Everything relied on me. I thought that by controlling everything, the operation would run more smoothly.

With every call, decision, and idea coming from me, I became my own bottleneck.

I realized that the problem was me. I was trying to do too much instead of delegating tasks effectively. I attempted to control every aspect of the business rather than letting go and allowing it to grow. I was focused on achieving specific results, but this became my downfall. All the outcomes depended on me rather than on others who could help solve these issues through leadership.

This phenomenon, which we call the "founder's trap," involves the tension between doing tasks ourselves versus delegating them. Many founders experience the struggle of determining what they should or shouldn't be doing. It's not just about handing off specific tasks; it's about relinquishing control.

Often, people mistakenly think delegation means simply passing off an email task or filling out a form to someone else. That's not the point. The real goal is to empower others to take control and own the results that they establish for themselves.

Most founders believe that delegation means assigning tasks to others. However, what we really want is to entrust the entire problem to other people. We should say, "Here is the issue we are facing, and I'm relying on you to think critically about how to best solve it."

We use an impact filter to facilitate this process. If you find yourself being the bottleneck, meaning you're the one completing every impact filter to tackle every problem in the business, you will continue to be overwhelmed. This is where the impact filter, mentioned in Chapter Four, becomes essential.

I've found that using an impact filter has significantly impacted my approach to leadership. The concept comes from

Dan Sullivan at Strategic Coach. The impact filter helps me empower others to think, build, and solve problems. When team members create solutions, they take ownership, making it more likely they will execute them effectively.

This process has compelled me to reflect on key questions: What is the purpose of this project? What are we aiming to achieve? Teresa Hanratty used to refer to it as the "purpose, process, and payoff." We need to define what success looks like, and this can be challenging. It's not simply about achieving better results; we need to envision the ideal outcomes.

We should consider the following: How should success be measured? Who will be involved? What specific tasks need to be done? Equally important is understanding what failure looks like. If we don't complete this project, or if we do it poorly, what will the consequences be? It's crucial to examine both sides of the equation when addressing problems.

When we use the impact filter, we often identify a major macro problem and then break it down into three specific initiatives tied to that problem. We assign each initiative's impact filter to different team members, often three or six people, who will work on it. Afterward, we consolidate everything into a single playbook to guide our execution over the next ninety days.

Once we've trained everyone on the impact filter and started implementing it, I've noticed a positive change. The leaders no longer check in with me constantly or hover around my office. They've begun to take ownership of problems, identify new challenges, and actively use the tools they've learned with others. This fosters a culture of problem-solving and decision-making, which is essential for scaling the business without my constant involvement.

Ultimately, this approach transforms the chaos of running a business into a well-oiled machine, enabling capable people to operate effectively without relying solely on me.

Turning ideas into outcomes is essential. Perhaps the most important aspect is transforming people who might typically be at your doorstep asking for solutions into problem solvers and leaders within the organization who can inspire others.

People often ask me about the real bottleneck. It's not about blaming people, including myself, but rather about identifying the actual constraint. What is the core issue? What is the bottleneck? If you've ever played Jenga, you'll know that just one piece of wood, when removed, can cause the entire structure to collapse. We refer to that as the bottleneck.

When addressing a business challenge, the first step is to understand what bottleneck you're trying to resolve. From there, you need to dig for a solution.

I find that good leaders approach problems differently from bad leaders. Bad leaders often justify poor results by pointing to external factors, like a bad market, vendor, or solution. In contrast, good leaders seek out others who have achieved better results and identify the underlying problems they can address. More often than not, the bottleneck turns out to be a systemic issue rather than a personal one, highlighting the need for extreme ownership. The mindset should be: *I am the problem. I am the solution.* The missing element often lies in that Jenga block.

Let me share a relevant story. AmeriLife's marketing department decided to add an AmeriLife company to all the affiliate firms the company had purchased. This occurred when a private equity firm purchased a 60 percent stake in the company, with AmeriLife serving as the sponsor. While someone had decided to add their name to ours, nobody was really asking what the unanticipated consequences of doing so would be.

I use a specific filter when addressing business challenges: not everything that feels good effectively solves a business problem. For instance, while someone might think we need a new computer system or CRM, the critical question is, "What business problem are we trying to solve?"

We should avoid making changes simply for the sake of novelty. Regarding the AmeriLife situation, someone in the leadership team believed that having an AmeriLife-related company would benefit us just because they owned a portion of our business. To assess this idea, I asked the CEO, "Is this critical, important, or merely nice to do?"

It's essential to prioritize the right problems when systematizing your business processes; otherwise, you risk not addressing issues that genuinely affect your profitability and growth. Here are the three categories of tasks:

1. Critical Tasks: These are non-negotiable. If you fail to address them, your profitability and growth plans may suffer significantly.
2. Important Tasks: While not immediately detrimental, overlooking these could gradually hurt your profits and overall business health in the long run.
3. Nice-to-Do Tasks: These may feel good to work on, but do not contribute significantly to increasing profits, production, or growth rates.

In a discussion with the CEO, I emphasized the importance of identifying which tasks fall into these categories. The primary focus needed to be on activities that enhance the brand, profitability, and growth, rather than pursuing an idea that is merely nice to consider.

Ultimately, the CEO agreed that some initiatives were nice to do but not essential. When building processes, it's crucial to focus solely on items that are critical to future growth and to discard those that are simply nice to have.

When a particular strategy or system proves successful, document and replicate it to protect that "magic." Conversely, if something isn't working, it should be eliminated from the system. You'll recognize inefficiencies when systems are created but remain unused: no one is engaging with or reporting on them.

More importantly, encourage others to create playbooks. A well-documented process is superior to relying on individual memory. Established processes eliminate confusion about previous decisions, since everything is clearly outlined.

When scaling your business, the priority should be to systematize all valuable knowledge, intellectual property, and contributions made by your team. Use tools like impact filters to regularly assess and enhance the most critical aspects of your business.

Yes, it's true: Rome wasn't built in a day. What I would suggest is identifying what we call "rocks," which are the three most critical challenges within your organization to focus on every ninety days. If you have fifteen problems, prioritize and address the top three first; the other twelve will have to wait.

You can start by listing all the issues and processes that need improvement, ranking them from one to fifteen. Once you identify the top three, develop systems and processes that integrate these solutions into the fabric of your organization. Implementing something new can be challenging and requires significant effort and communication, often tenfold.

However, once the new processes are in place and everyone is up to speed, it will feel like they've always been part of your operations. By tackling three major challenges every ninety days, you will eventually find that while there may still be around twenty-two problems, they will be less impactful, as most of the critical issues have already been resolved. It's about removing the "Jenga blocks" within the company.

I think Jay-Z famously said that he has ninety-nine problems. I've read business books that mention there are always twenty-two problems, and others suggest there are twenty-three. What I do know is that every company, regardless of its size, has problems.

All of these problems represent opportunities. The key question is whether you can identify the most critical ones. "What business challenges are we trying to solve?"

Focus on identifying the three most critical problems and work on those. If you've ever worked for a large or even a small company, you may have felt puzzled about how it functions. It can often feel like a house of cards. I used to work at American Express Financial Advisors, which is a part of American Express, and I often thought, *These people can't even manage the basics. How are they growing by 25 percent per year?*

Then it dawned on me that I was looking for perfection within the system instead of recognizing that the company's culture was driving those impressive results. There will never be a perfect system, and organizations are always evolving as they strive to reach the next level. This is simply part of the growth process for any business.

How can you tell if the team is relying too much on memory? One indicator is when people frequently ask questions like, "What did we decide about this or that?"

For instance, they might ask, "What did we decide about the scorecard?" or "What are the criteria for getting promoted or expanding control?" Similarly, they could inquire about the bonus schedule for incentives. If these questions arise, it usually means a decision has been made. However, although it might be documented somewhere, the need to ask indicates it hasn't been communicated effectively.

In other words, communication needs to be a priority. If a decision is made but is not consistently presented to the team every week, whether in a meeting, through a memo, or as part of standard operating procedures, it isn't fully ingrained in the team's understanding. When people continually ask, "What did we decide about this?" or "What did we decide about that?" it signals a communication gap on my part.

For example, we have something called an "out-of-office contract." This contract applies to people who require less leadership because they essentially run their own business within our organization. People used to bombard me with emails asking, "What are the criteria for an out-of-office contract?" I would receive five or six inquiries a week!

To address this, I began including the criteria in our weekly call, which everyone in the firm attends, and we also made announcements during that time. I specifically set aside a section to explain how to qualify for the out-of-office contract. Every week, I remind everyone of the criteria.

Another common question I get is about our performance measurement grid, which rewards increased production with higher compensation, a system we refer to as "do more, get more." I include information about this grid in the announcements as well. I remind the team that we have two measurement periods: January 31 and July 1. It's crucial to keep an eye on their business results to determine whether they qualify for a higher position on the grid.

Ultimately, if you're not communicating effectively, it often points to a need for better clarity and consistency. Consider how you can present information regularly so everyone stays informed.

The most important system to implement is a leadership development plan that addresses span-of-control issues. This is the number one priority for ensuring that everyone understands their role in growing and developing other leaders.

The second-most crucial system is a scorecard. When you're developing leaders, it's essential to track what they're developing into and measure the results you want to achieve.

By year eight, it's vital to have financial controls in place. Understanding the flow of money, what's coming in and going out, is a critical aspect of managing a business.

It's important to distinguish between cash flow and profit, as many people often confuse the two. This confusion can hinder your ability to manage a margin-based business effectively. For instance, you could generate $5 million in annual revenue but only make $150,000 in profit. While that might seem successful, it's simply a cycle of money coming in and out, reflecting a lack of understanding of your margins.

To be serious about growth and expansion, you need to establish financial controls by year five. This will help you make informed investments and ensure a sustainable business model.

The root cause of most issues usually involves people. When building a system, it's essential to focus on two key metrics: activity and conversion. Activity measures how many times we're performing certain actions, while conversion indicates how many actions we need to take to achieve a desired result. It's important to categorize these metrics effectively, typically into five or six areas related to conversion and activity.

To analyze the system, I start by looking at the result. If the desired outcome, such as a close ratio, isn't being met, I first examine the presentation that preceded it. If the presentation is solid, I then look at the prior meeting, such as the introductory meeting. If that meeting is also satisfactory, I investigate the origin of the lead.

This structured approach helps identify bottlenecks in the process. The key to finding these bottlenecks is digging deep into the work. If you look closely enough, you'll uncover one or two factors that are negatively impacting the metrics.

We follow a principle known as "inspect what you expect." When results are not as anticipated, one of the best ways to identify and solve the problem is through observation. I often sit down with the person involved and use the two most powerful words in leadership: "Show me." This approach prompts them to physically demonstrate each step in the process, rather than telling me what they think I want to hear. This hands-on demonstration quickly reveals breakdowns in the process.

PHASE
Four

*(Others start
building inside what you built.)*

Chapter 10

REBUILD THE VISION

We are now entering phase four of the business, a stage we refer to as the "platform flip." This is a significant moment when you transition from being the sole leader and decision-maker in your organization to establishing a business that can thrive independently. At this point, your organization will begin to take on a life of its own and start to grow without your constant involvement.

Every founder reaches a pivotal moment when they realize that their influence, strategy, work ethic, and integrity have helped build a strong enough talent pool. This talent allows the business, initially reliant on you, to become a self-sustaining engine. You've created an infrastructure with leaders and departments, effectively managing the span of control and fostering leadership development.

As your teams grow, everything begins to align, making your presence less critical than it once was. Essentially, you have built a business that can build other businesses, an organization that encourages career development and teamwork toward common goals, all without needing your direct input.

This is the "flip," and it's when the positive transformation begins. Looking back, you'll see that the organization has adopted its own personality, one that reflects your original vision without requiring your daily involvement. The pitch decks and presentations are now crafted by others who share your core values, and you no longer need to approve them. At this point, your company represents the vision you had from the beginning, rather than being a product of your constant oversight.

However, many businesses encounter a challenge at this phase. The vision and mission that you originally established, which have successfully guided your company thus far, may not be sufficient to propel it to the next level. As your business evolves, you must adapt your strategies to ensure continued growth and success. You cannot scale a company indefinitely with the same old strategies without reassessing what needs to change and how to achieve that. It's natural to outgrow your initial vision, and recognizing this is crucial to ongoing development.

As you grow your business, you will inevitably need to reinvent yourself. The best companies continuously challenge their current practices and question the status quo. Those who cannot keep their eyes open and reimagine what their business will look like in the future will ultimately struggle or fail. We are currently experiencing this as we assess the future of our organization. Despite our success, we are asking ourselves whether we can continue to grow and expand at the same rate we have in the past.

Every business owner who has scaled a business knows that it is often easier to establish it than to sustain aggressive year-over-year growth with the same strategies. So, what are the biggest challenges? In many cases, it's what you've built.

You have likely aligned everyone around a scorecard and are moving in the same direction toward achieving common objectives. However, as your organization has grown, it has become more controlled. You may have eliminated discretion at the operational level, leading to a situation where everyone strictly follows procedures and policies. This structure can create a cage that limits your ability to expand your mindset.

You may notice this limitation as you think back over the years, eight, nine, ten, and beyond. As humans, we tend to romanticize our past. We recall how we used to buy lunch for the team every day or how we stayed up late to fix the copier to print documents for an important meeting. We remember working on a case until it was a fun challenge, whatever it took to succeed.

The issue isn't the nostalgia for that vision, a past we appreciate and often reflect on. While those experiences have led us to our current situation, they won't suffice for scaling the business in the future. This isn't merely a romanticization of the past; it is a tendency for people to protect it rather than focus on the future. We must consider the unintended consequences of failing to adapt to change.

What are the roadblocks to anticipating the future? What if we're no longer here to protect what we've built? What happens when we're gone?

These limiting factors can undermine a business. To thrive, you must rewrite your vision. You need to think differently and demonstrate to others that a new direction for the future is in their best interest. This shift is essential for the company's growth and for everyone to achieve what they desire. This means establishing a new mission, a revitalized vision, a fresh way of thinking, a different market, a new territory, or a new product rather than continuing with the status quo. Change is necessary.

Believe me, we've all witnessed businesses that were once very successful but refused to adapt. On the other hand, we also see businesses thriving because they have embraced change. Take Netflix as a prime example.

Originally, Netflix operated similarly to Redbox, which offered DVD rentals through the mail. Redbox became known for its convenience, allowing customers to rent DVDs without the frustrations of going to a Blockbuster, where popular titles were often out of stock or where you had to wait in long lines. Plus, if you returned a movie late, you could end up paying more than the cost of the rental.

However, Reed Hastings, the CEO of Netflix, recognized that the DVD rental business would eventually decline. He saw streaming as the future. Instead of remaining in the DVD business, Netflix transitioned to an entirely new model focused on streaming content. Today, Netflix is a leading entertainment provider, known for binge-watching and original content.

In contrast, consider Sears. Once a successful catalog company, you could even buy a house through a Sears catalog. However, they failed to adapt to changing market demands, which contributed to their decline.

Now look at Amazon. Everyone knows Jeff Bezos started it in his garage as an online bookstore that distributed books worldwide. Now, I don't know about you, but we receive so many Amazon packages at our house that we've jokingly named it "Amazon-esia." It feels like Christmas every single day, filled with things we didn't even know we ordered. Just think about the data Amazon consumes through its web services and what the future holds, such as drones.

What's the point? Great companies, the ones that last a lifetime, have founders and leaders willing to think innovatively. They challenge current assumptions and seek a future because they recognize that without evolution, their businesses will stagnate.

It's time to reframe our vision, Vision 2.0. At Florida Financial Advisors, we gather everyone in a room and consistently challenge one another to think about what comes next. You can't scale a platform or grow aggressively using the same old playbook.

In our case, it all started with my wife playfully criticizing me at our bar after a day of drinking. Years eight through ten mean it's time to get serious about all the things we haven't done within our business. Leaders need to inspire and build more within the organization.

When we achieve success, we can envision how many more leaders we'll develop, the markets we'll enter, the revenue we'll generate, and the products and stock options we can offer. This ongoing evolution is crucial.

It's time to reframe, recast, and reinvent. We need to dismantle some of the old playbooks to create new ones and update our scorecards. We should create new roles, infrastructure, and challenges for the next chapter.

When faced with pushback regarding our vision, we must help people understand that the original vision still exists. We're not discarding it; we're expanding it. We're looking toward the next generation of leaders, products, markets, and opportunities because now we're a platform.

Platforms will always need visionaries and leaders who can foresee the future, especially in this age of rapid technological advancement. We must take advantage of these innovations and apply them to our systems to remain competitive and continue growing at our desired rates.

Most importantly, when this progress occurs, those who embrace this vision will not only improve their lives and careers but will also join us on this journey rather than resisting the natural evolution of our field.

There are a few important points to discuss. First, effective leaders have the crucial responsibility of anticipating the future before it arrives. Their role is to look around corners and see what others might not yet recognize.

For us, growth is viewed as a mathematical formula. A significant part of this involves hiring the right people, making them productive, onboarding, training, offboarding when necessary, and ultimately developing them into leaders. If our goal is to grow by 60 percent each year, we must calculate the necessary revenue projections and the infrastructure needed to achieve that growth.

As I analyzed the numbers, it became clear that our growth would plateau or stagnate unless we made a significant leap. Many businesses transition from a scrappy, hands-on approach to stagnation, often resulting in growth targets of only 10 percent, 15 percent, or 20 percent per year. This is usually due to the limitations of the established playbook.

I realize that the way we currently operate, our methods for recruiting, training, and developing people, will not sustain our growth in 2028, which is just two years away. This insight makes me anxious, prompting me to think about alternative strategies in the financial services sector. I also consider what our competitors do; even if their profit margins are not as high, their volume may help us compensate and enhance our existing strategy for growth.

Ultimately, it's essential to continuously forecast where you want to grow, determine your desired growth rate, and identify the infrastructure needed to support it. Additionally, it's important to explore new ways to accelerate that journey, finding innovative paths to achieve your long-term vision while avoiding stagnation in the business.

Well, there are two parts of that, right?

What if you were to pursue a shiny object, only to discover that it was the wrong one to chase? For instance, consider what would have happened if Blockbuster Video had concluded that Redbox was the future and had followed its lead, ultimately leading to its downfall. In this scenario, Redbox had already pivoted to streaming and evolved into Netflix. Essentially, by mistakenly thinking you were chasing a competitor, you may inadvertently lead your business astray, as the true competitor will have already moved ahead and found success in a different direction.

To move forward effectively, it's crucial to be strategic without abandoning your existing vision, whether that's version 0.1 or 1.0. Many organizations make the mistake of trying to transition directly from 1.0 to 2.0 by discarding 1.0 entirely.

For instance, a company like ours, which focuses on hiring, recruiting, and training new talent, might decide to stop those practices and only pursue experienced individuals. They might aim to recruit a handful of exceptional talents, like "twenty Tom Bradys." However, this approach often reveals that they lack the necessary infrastructure, talent, technology, and leadership capabilities. As a result, they could take a significant step backward, and in some cases, even risk going out of business. Companies that make such drastic shifts sometimes become acquisition targets.

It's essential when energizing people about 2.0 that we still maintain what made us successful in 1.0. We are not replacing one version with the other; instead, we envision it more like a pyramid. Version 1.0 serves as the foundation, and we build on top of it with version 2.0 to promote growth and expansion. Similarly, version 3.0 will be added on top of 2.0, and so forth, while still preserving the foundational elements of version 1.0.

We are not abandoning the strategies that led to our success; rather, we are enhancing them by integrating new strategies alongside the old ones. Our goal is to evolve by building on what has already worked for us.

There are two main points I want to address. Often, when people struggle to define their vision, they mistakenly believe that outside consultants with MBAs can create a better strategy than the people who are already in the business. In my experience, whenever companies hire consultants who have never worked in that business or who weren't there from the beginning, trying to redefine the future usually ends in disaster.

Consultants just can't grasp the intricacies of the work in a six- or nine-month project well enough to accurately define a business's future. On the other hand, I believe that coaching can exponentially enhance personal growth. If you want to progress significantly from where you currently are, the key is your personal development, and coaching plays a major role in that.

It's crucial to distinguish between coaching and consulting. Coaching involves working with people who have achieved greater success than you and paying them for their insights, advice, and strategies to overcome the challenges you face.

However, not all coaching is effective. You must evaluate the coaching you receive through the lens of your specific situation and context. Ultimately, as a founder, it's your responsibility to determine which advice resonates with you and to trust your instincts, as they have guided you thus far.

At the same time, you need to be open and humble enough to acknowledge that there are people who may excel in areas where you do not. Often, those people who can support you, whether through feedback, relationship building, or even financial investment, are willing to share their experiences.

One thing I've learned over the years is that everyone aspires to be a person of interest. Deep down, we all want to matter to someone. This fundamental desire means that by choosing the right coaches, you can gain invaluable insights, as people are often eager to share what they know to feel that sense of significance.

I assure you that the lessons you learn from these individuals will be invaluable to your life and career, provided you can set aside your ego, listen carefully, and remain open to feedback and coaching from others.

It's essential to choose coaches who are more accomplished than you are. One significant challenge I've encountered is receiving advice from those whose perspective is smaller than mine. Their understanding of future challenges and vision is often limited by their own experiences.

As you grow, it's important to recognize that you may outgrow your coaches. Therefore, it's vital to continue seeking out coaches who can challenge you and have achieved things you have not yet accomplished, yet who are still willing to share their insights to help you reach the next level.

Chapter 11

EXIT OPTIONAL

After achieving a level of success you never thought possible, with a business that runs itself, there comes a moment when you could simply walk away. People will ask you, "Why don't you just sell your business? Why do you continue to work?"

The amazing part is that when you have a platform business, you can leave, and it will still grow without you. It will continue to evolve, produce significant results, and have a massive impact on people's lives. Leaders will be created.

You have built not just a job but a sustainable business. You've navigated the challenges and gone through the process of business building. Now you find yourself in a position where your exit is optional. You could wrap things up today, cash a substantial check, and move on, but you choose not to.

Unfortunately, most businesses never reach this level of growth, where the exit becomes optional. Many businesses achieve decent income but ultimately suffer a slow decline because their leaders maintain too much control, which leads to boredom and burnout. This can cause the business to quietly fizzle out.

We've all witnessed this, whether it's local stores, pizza shops, or dry cleaners. A once-thriving business, initially started with enthusiasm, eventually declines. Floors go unrepaired, bathrooms aren't cleaned, windows become scratched, and before long, the business that was once successful is no longer viable. Burnout is the common factor that kills companies that fail to pursue the ultimate goal: to become a platform where exiting is optional.

As you think about your business, consider what happens when you achieve scale. Platforms have the potential to continue growing.

People continue to grow, even without your direct involvement. That's when the shift begins, and suddenly, you find everything working in your favor. That's the essence of legacy.

It's at this moment that you realize that you don't run the business; the business runs itself. You're no longer needed to show up every day.

Now, you have a choice to make: Do you want to keep it going? Are you ready to embrace Vision 2.0?

The beauty of this situation is that you are in control. Someone once told me that retirement isn't about stopping work; it's about reaching a point where work becomes optional, and everything you've ever wanted in life becomes affordable. This realization allows you to make decisions about the next chapter of your life.

Do you want to be the king of kings, the kingmaker? Do you want to become a builder of builders? Do you want to teach others how to create a business? Would you prefer to distill your experiences into something valuable to sell? Many successful people move on to establish coaching businesses, offering their playbooks, leadership models, and cultural insights. They provide their blueprints and platforms.

This is where the pivot happens; you get to decide where to take it from here.

I'm involved in several of these aspects. Today, my business has expanded to a level I never imagined. I typically have only about seven emails in my inbox, I don't receive countless phone calls every day, and my calendar features just two or three meetings that I schedule myself. This gives me the time I need to think and grow.

So, what do I want to do next? I have a couple of initiatives underway. One is called "Take the Power Back," which aims to change the narrative surrounding Gen Z and support young entrepreneurs. We provide leadership, vision, and access to resources that help them achieve their goals.

Additionally, we've started a licensing deal as a way to grow our business into FFA 2.0. This initiative allows others to create their own individual businesses, which can be sold. We take an equity stake in our intellectual property and offer it to them. Then, as they expand, we help them develop, using the same platform we have, enabling us to reach different markets more quickly.

Lastly, I've started a restaurant, even though I have no previous experience in the restaurant business. It's a challenging industry with thin profit margins and demands significant effort and energy. In the worst-case scenario, it will be a cool place where I can eat with my friends and call my own. I envision it being beautiful, with great food.

I also started a property casualty business. Once you reach a point where work becomes optional, life opens up, and you have the freedom to make your own choices. That's where your legacy begins.

For most founders who achieve success with a platform business, real legacy is about what happens when you can completely remove yourself from it. You definitely don't want to think that if you walked away, the business would fall apart. Legacies are built on strong foundations.

Ultimately, that's what makes a business unstoppable. You can invest your time and energy and decide whether you want to be involved. When the business is structured correctly, you don't exit because you're burned out; you exit when you choose to, on your own terms. That's truly the best part about building and scaling a business.

I've heard people say, "I could be successful, but I don't want to work that hard." However, this is a misunderstanding. The most successful people often have the flexibility to do whatever they want. The real question is whether they develop themselves enough to build something significant and lasting that benefits everyone while also achieving what they desire.

Someone once told me that you will selfishly get whatever you want when you unselfishly do things for others without expecting anything in return. It's only through serving others with a mindset of generosity that you can achieve this. Ultimately, the choice is yours.

To prevent business burnout, there are three key strategies to consider:

1. Develop Others: One major cause of burnout is the inability to develop others who can help and ultimately replace you. By mentoring and training your team, you reduce your workload and build a more sustainable business.

2. Systematize Processes: It's crucial to systematize every procedure, including the development of leaders. When you find yourself repeating the same tasks endlessly, it can become overwhelming and lead to resentment. By creating systems, you streamline operations and free up time for more valuable activities.

3. Schedule Your Priorities: Failing to prioritize your schedule can lead to burnout. Trying to be all things to all people is unsustainable. Identify the key drivers of your business and make it a point to schedule your time around your goals and core values. This focus will help you avoid burnout and maintain a fulfilling work-life balance.

Once you've achieved certain levels of success, however you choose to measure that, people are naturally drawn to understanding how you did it. I often have lunch calls with individuals in our network, ranging from party and event planners to medical device salespeople.

Business is business, and the formula remains the same: have a compelling vision, sell that vision from the outset, and focus on developing leaders, again and again. It's also essential to maintain a scorecard and drive that scorecard all the way to the finish line.

We've created an internal platform within our business that allows people to brand their own organizations, retain full ownership, and use our infrastructure. They can also replicate our systems and processes, enabling them to build their futures and fortunes while leveraging the capabilities we've already established. That's the power of our platform.

We are the "kingmakers." If you develop your skills and replicate the same systems, you can achieve the same results while still owning your business.

Recently, we've also entered into licensing agreements with people who run similar yet stagnant businesses and want to achieve substantial growth. We've invited them to join us, offering our intellectual property and coaching in exchange for a percentage of their future sales.

I also provide coaching and mentoring to friends and contacts who frequently ask for guidance on various situations. This is a regular part of my routine. Given that my network is heavily focused on financial services, both within and outside our company, I'm just a phone call away for those seeking advice.

Recently, I connected with a guy I hired twenty-five years ago. After some successful exits with another business, he bought a financial advisory firm and reached out for suggestions on accelerating its growth. This led us to sign a licensing deal with his business, transforming our relationship into a new business opportunity. More importantly, the knowledge he gains from this will significantly increase his potential returns upon exiting.

I learned something important a long time ago. Larry Post once told me, "The weak protect." If there's one message I want people to take away from this, it's that if you try to protect everything you own out of fear that someone else might do something better than you, you end up creating your own cage.

The idea of giving to receive is powerful and has biblical roots, similar to the Pareto principle and the golden rule. Most importantly, don't hoard your possessions or knowledge to keep others from having what you have. Instead, teach them how to achieve what you've accomplished.

Ultimately, by sharing what you know and helping others succeed, you also pave the way to your own success.

There are a couple of things I realized when my business could function without me. One of them involved one of our top executives, Victoria Rapp, who was previously known as Victoria Pena. She started as an intern and had progressed through nearly every role in the company. She was a recruiter, an onboarder, and a receptionist, and now she leads a team of sixty people as our chief operating officer. She has done an amazing job. What began as a casual relationship of grabbing beers after work and sharing lunch every day has evolved into a deeper partnership.

Recently, we faced a situation, and I asked why she hadn't brought it to my attention. She explained, "I want you to know that I consciously avoid bringing you problems I know I'm empowered to fix."

At that moment, I realized that when your leadership team can handle day-to-day challenges independently, it indicates that you've reached a significant milestone in your organization. They don't need you, and, frankly, they don't want you interfering.

How does that make me feel? I have mixed emotions. As the founder, I want to feel relevant and believe I still provide value. Also, a part of me misses the feeling of being needed within the organization.

Today, I find myself meddling in various issues just to feel impactful. I pick a problem, a person, or a process to get involved in so I can continue contributing and feel valued. Sometimes, my leaders tell me I distract them from solving their own problems, which they have already been working on, and that my involvement can complicate things.

But that's okay; as a founder, I still get to exercise my influence and engage as I choose, even if it's better for me to step back. I do this because I have a personal desire to feel needed and appreciated within the organization.

CONCLUSION

First, thank you for reading this and for purchasing the book. I appreciate your commitment to pursuing your dreams of becoming a business owner, creating your own job, providing employment for others, and building a business and a platform.

I hope you realize that you've always been the platform behind this business. You are the one who endured the grind, who persevered through tough times, and who took on the various roles of building, shipping, accounting, cleaning, marketing, and everything else. You've weathered chaos and scaling challenges; you've done it all. From creating systems to overcoming setbacks and celebrating breakthroughs, your journey has been remarkable.

But the key takeaway I want you to remember is that it was never just about business; it was really about becoming the type of person who can build one. Success isn't solely about hiring the perfect team or crafting the ideal business plan. It's not about finding the right industry or choosing the perfect career path. It's about your personal growth, creating a vision, and establishing the daily habits necessary to prioritize what truly matters.

You need the ability to cultivate growth in others, becoming a kingmaker who helps people build robust systems, processes, and playbooks. This involves capturing your knowledge and making everything systematic while pushing through that difficult grind when you question whether you'll ever succeed or find ease in your business.

That's the essence of the message. Ultimately, a platform is created by founders with great intentions. However, the ones who truly realize those intentions are those who are sincerely committed to their own growth.

Thank you for striving for more, for taking the time to read this book, and for investing whatever you paid for it. I also appreciate you choosing to engage with this content rather than binge-watching Netflix or endlessly scrolling through Instagram or TikTok. You have choices, and I want to express my gratitude to you for choosing to embark on this journey with me as you become a platform.

THANK YOU FOR READING MY BOOK!

Just to say thanks for buying and reading my book,
I would like to give you a few free bonus gifts,
no strings attached!

Scan the QR Code:

*I appreciate your interest in my book and value your feedback,
as it helps me improve future versions.
I would appreciate it if you could leave your invaluable
review on Amazon.com with your feedback.
Thank you!*

www.ingramcontent.com/pod-product-compliance
Lightning Source LLC
Chambersburg PA
CBHW061313280526
45784CB00002B/978